RECORD-BR
BRITAIN

PETER NALDRETT

Thanks as always to Nicola, Toby and Willow for coming along
to enjoy the whizzes, thrills and adrenaline rushes.

Dedicated to the memory of Michele Vincent, who worked with me
on the Rotherham Advertiser back in the day and is very much missed.

CONWAY
Bloomsbury Publishing Plc
50 Bedford Square, London, WC1B 3DP, UK
Bloomsbury Publishing Ireland Limited
29 Earlsfort Terrace, Dublin 2, D02 AY28, Ireland

BLOOMSBURY, CONWAY and the Conway logo are trademarks of Bloomsbury Publishing Plc

First published in Great Britain 2025

A catalogue record for this book is available from the British Library

Library of Congress Cataloguing-in-Publication data has been applied for

ISBN: PB: 978-1-8448-6694-6; ePub: 978-1-8448-6697-7; ePDF: 978-1-8448-6695-3

2 4 6 8 10 9 7 5 3 1

Design by Lee-May Lim

Typeset in Brandon Grotesque by Tom Storr

Printed and bound in Dubai by Oriental Press

To find out more about our authors and books visit www.bloomsbury.com and sign up for our newsletters

For product safety related questions contact productsafety@bloomsbury.com

RECORD-BREAKING
BRITAIN

101 OF BRITAIN'S BIGGEST, SMALLEST, OLDEST, FASTEST, TALLEST, MOST FUN DAYS OUT

PETER NALDRETT

CONWAY

LONDON · OXFORD · NEW YORK · NEW DELHI · SYDNEY

LONDON

18
23
24
17
25
28
30
22
29
31
19
26/27
21
20

92/93
89/90/91
88
85
86/87
82
83 84
81
78 79
77
80
76 74 75
72
73
68
71 69
70
54 67
57 63/64 65
52 55 60 66
44 61/62
45 48 59
43 46/47 56 101
49 50 41 58
51 40
53 42
39
38
11 12
37
10
35 33
6 2 7 34
9 8 32
36
15 13 14
4 16
3
5
1

96
99
98
94
97
95
100

CONTENTS

FOREWORD

I'm a huge fan of a day out. I mean, who isn't? As a kid, trips to the local leisure centre (Herringthorpe, epic wave machine circa 1982), park and cricket club were treasured alongside days out on the train to the seaside with ham sandwiches to go with chips, bought when we got there and eaten sitting on a sea wall.

I remember my first theme park trip to Alton Towers. Alongside my friend Joanne, I screamed on the Corkscrew and wandered through the gardens. It stuck with me so much that years later, when the time came to pick a honeymoon destination Alton Towers won over the Seychelles. Young and in love, my new hubby and I snogged on the Oblivion as we faced our future together. Perhaps it was some sort of metaphor. Whatever, we still go there annually and hold hands all these years later.

The arrival of children meant more days out but this time with family, including extended family. With a variety of ages and preferences to cater for, we were searching for ways to keep most, if not all, happy.

And here is where a book like this is invaluable. Pete has done the hard work for us. There's something here to suit everyone from adventurous grannies to timid cousins. With helpful facts and figures to ease the organising, this book provides the best advice for those seeking meaningful and memory-making distraction attractions.

So, whether it's Lee Valley Water Park or Tooting Bec Lido, there's something here for all tastes and abilities. Why not see how many you can tick off?

Reverend Kate Bottley

INTRODUCTION

Tackling adrenaline-fuelled, record-breaking activities around Britain invoked a range of exciting and satisfying emotions in me, but of all those, the anticipation beforehand was most unexpected.

That feeling as I stood in a queue waiting to go on the country's fastest roller coaster, seeing the ride start dozens of times. Hearing the screams. Seeing the faces as they emerged from the ride. The nerves of being secured in my seat before heading into the longest coaster ride, the seemingly endless climb up the track high above Blackpool's skyline. Taking my solo seat and knowing I was about to be dangled by a wire, then lowered down into a huge cavern with our tallest waterfall crashing around my head. And I'll not forget the beating of my heart as I stared off the top of a Welsh mountain, secured to the fastest zip line about to fly through the air at 100mph.

Matching these heightened emotions was the thrill of completing the challenge, being able to say, 'I did it!' and, in some cases, conquering fears.

Being a record breaker, of course, is not always about inducing adrenaline and completing tough challenges at high speed. There are also lots of activities in this book which are thought-provoking and don't need a huge amount of physical exertion. You can, it turns out, be a record-breaker by taking an inspiring stroll or exploring a renowned building.

So what is it about record-breaking activities that make them so appealing and addictive?

Well, for me, if you're going to get a view over London there's no point going to the second highest observation deck to enjoy it. 'I climbed the second highest mountain in Scotland' doesn't really cut the cheese, does it? If you're going to do something exciting, you may as well max out on the challenge and bag the bragging rights that go with it.

And so, yes, I wanted to see the biggest cave entrance, not just any old cave entrance. I wanted to experience the darkest skies in the UK, not just see a few stars. I wanted a tour around the largest cathedral, sing the Christmas carols few people have ever heard, taste an ice cream from the largest parlour, learn in the oldest museum, climb the tallest mountains, cycle the longest incline, tackle the toughest white water, laugh and be inspired at the world's largest arts festival. Many of these record-breaking days out will cost relatively little, but deliver big rewards.

If you want to tick off this collection of extreme activities, you're going to have to show some serious commitment. In the words of the late Roy Castle, 'dedication's what you need' if you want to complete these 101 record-breaking challenges in Britain. But if you do tick them all off, you certainly win the right to blow your own trumpet.

Peter Naldrett

001

BE THE MOST SOUTHERLY PERSON ON MAINLAND BRITAIN

Latitude
49° 57' 30" N

Wildlife to spot
seals, basking sharks, porpoises, dolphins

Tech highlight
Marconi's radio experiments

Cornish translation of 'The Lizard'
An Lysardh

LIZARD POINT
CORNWALL

When looking for extreme challenges to complete, some adventurous folk take on the ultimate north-south British journey and leave John O'Groats in Scotland for Cornwall's Land's End. Some walk, some cycle, some run. Many drop out. Land's End is traditionally seen as the most extreme tip of Cornwall and so the furthest you can go. But it's not the southernmost point in Britain. To stand on a clifftop safe in the knowledge that nobody in Britain can be further south than you, follow the coast inland from Land's End – to Lizard Point. Here, you can look out to the waves crashing on the rocks below and drink in the fresh air at one of the few places in our country to sit south of the 50°N line of latitude. Have a picture taken as the most southerly person in Britain!

To get here, turn south from Helston and travel along the Lizard Peninsula until you reach Lizard Village. From here, it's a short walk or drive to Lizard Point. It seems like everything around here is called Lizard something or other. Lizard Village is a good place to park up. There are a couple of good pubs here, the chip shop is worth writing home about, and you've simply got to pay a visit to Ann's Pasties. Many connoisseurs of the Cornish Pasty will tell you these are the finest in all the county. They used to be sold out of a house on a side street, but have since moved to a bigger spot with a bar in the main square. Grabbing a large traditional Cornish and taking it to munch down at Lizard Point is highly recommended. All told, the small Lizard Village punches well above its weight when it comes to facilities, the reason largely being down to the

geographical landmark pulling in visitors. Within walking distance of Lizard Point, Lizard Lighthouse shines every evening and will also blast out its foghorn in low visibility. During daylight hours you can grab a tour of the tower and take a souvenir home from the shop. The old lighthouse keeper's cottages are available as holiday lets if you would like to stay in this special place longer. Walk on footpaths from the lighthouse across clifftop fields to reach the National Trust's Lizard Wireless Station. It was in these humble surroundings that Italian inventor Guglielmo Marconi carried out pioneering wireless experiments at the turn of the 20th century.

When you're exploring the Lizard Peninsula, pay close attention to the rock, because it's unusual and you'll find locally crafted gifts made out of it. In particular, the dark green, smooth rock called Serpentine is a Cornish favourite and special to these parts. It looks so unusual, so waxy and exquisite, you'll be able to recognise it with no problem. In fact, it looks like snake skin. Funny that. It was originally formed deep beneath the surface of Earth in the continental crust and has been pushed upwards by slowly-moving tectonic plates over millions of years. Rich in magnesium and iron, it's used for building materials as well as ornaments. But I think it looks best in situ in the Cornish cliffs.

002

STRIDE OUT ONTO BRITAIN'S LENGTHIEST LONG-DISTANCE FOOTPATH

Length 1,014km (630 miles)

Highest point Great Hangman 318m (1,043ft)

Steepest section 8,000 step climb at Clovelly

Counties it crosses 4

Number of stiles and gates approx. 2,500

SOUTH WEST COAST PATH

Strap on those walking boots, get your O.S. map in hand and explore some of the best coastline in the world. Rugged cliffs with waves crashing on them, cool dudes surfing and some impressive sandy beaches; these are just some of the joys that await walkers stepping out on the challenging 1,014km (630 miles) South West Coast Path that starts in Minehead, Somerset, and meanders along the edge of the land all the way round to Poole Harbour, Dorset. The sheer size of this stunning long-distance walking path makes it as brutal as it is beautiful, and that's why the vast majority of people will dip into the route one day at a time rather than aiming to finish it all in one crazy, if magnificent, adventure.

I've completed long-distance routes before and know only too well that if you do it all in one go you are definitely going to encounter days when the weather and your own body are telling you to pack up, go home and have a nice, long bath. It takes a great deal of commitment to see out some of the much shorter long-distance routes, but a trek of this severity can easily eat into a couple of months. And so the challenge I'm throwing down for this record-breaking path is not necessarily to complete it within a certain timeframe. Tens of thousands of walkers use this route every year, and although a few hardy hikers will take on the whole of the long-distance path in one go, it's also a lot of fun to dip into it for a few hours at a time. You should aim to visit different sections of the path, enjoy coastal walks in different counties and get to the know the diverse scenery to be found in this most magical of seaside settings. Having said

that, if you do attempt to swallow the whole 630-mile path in one sitting, I'll definitely be in awe of you!

No matter which section of the South West Coast Path you attempt first, be it the northern coast of Cornwall or the southern route in Devon, you'll be made aware that this gargantuan adventure is now considered to be one big route. Similarities in the signage is a common thread all along the route. You'll see information boards putting your small section into a larger context. Get chatting to people you meet along the way and you'll discover folk attempting it all at once and people dividing it up into fun weekends away.

So where to go if you're just dipping into this record-breaking long-distance path? Well, the Jurassic Coast is an unmissable section, and a

great one to start with, down in Dorset. Perhaps plan a day walk around the stunning natural arch called Durdle Door and nearby Lulworth Cove. Further west along the southern coast, time your walk to take in beautiful St Michael's Mount on its own tidal island accessed from Marazion. Heading to the tip of Cornwall, there are some amazing walks to be done on the Lizard Peninsula, including paying a visit to the unforgettable Kynance Cove. The northern coast serves similarly enticing treats; definitely plan a route that takes in the magical Tintagel, legendary birthplace of King Arthur and location of the cave that Merlin supposedly occupied. And then, to complete your taster of the South West Coast Path, enjoy the amazing views of coast and moorland in Exmoor, where you can also spot red deer and the famous Exmoor Ponies.

003

Plant species
1,000+

Temperatures
reaching 35°C

Need for a coat
negligible

GO EXPLORING IN THE WORLD'S LARGEST INDOOR RAINFOREST

THE EDEN PROJECT CORNWALL

The futuristic domes of Cornwall's Eden Project have an air of otherworldly terraforming. Once you're inside them, you'll see the scale of what they've achieved here is mesmerising; over 1,000 different plants which are thriving in climatic conditions not normally found on our soil. Of the two biomes created here, it is the domed rainforest structure which is most fascinating and holds the record for being the largest in the world.

For over a century, the land housing this flagship of redevelopment was used as a china clay pit and had another-worldly, lunar landscape. Indeed, it was used as the planet Magrathea in the TV adaptation of *Hitchhiker's Guide to the Galaxy*. But by the mid-1990s, the pit was exhausted and abandoned. Work began in 1998 to create the innovative environmental visitor centre the Eden Project has become. With the visitor centre opening in 2000 and the first plants arriving shortly after, the full opening came in 2001. Since then, the Eden Project has dazzled visitors with its two

huge indoor biomes that recreate conditions in different parts of the world. The site has also become a venue for outdoor cinema screenings and music concerts during the summer. But for many people attending this popular Cornish visitor attraction, the favourite part of the day will be exploring a hot, steamy tropical rainforest environment and learning about the issues affecting such a biodiverse ecosystem.

Stepping into the Rainforest Biome is like journeying down to Brazil and enjoying the wonders of the Amazon; but you don't have to

pay the airfare, you can come back after an hour, and while you're there you can also enjoy the delicacies of an artisan lunch in the café. Joking aside, experiencing the Eden Project's rainforest doesn't pretend to match the real thing. Of course it doesn't. But there is a great amount of joy to be had in entering the largest indoor rainforest which has been built at the Eden Project. You'll be experiencing the soaring heat, sweating through the humidity, seeing the tropical flora and learning about the rubber and palm oil trade. Some of the plants you'll see there are simply mind-blowing. Pineapples growing at your feet, bananas hanging from the trees, sugar cane beside the path you are guided around on. It's a bombardment of the senses, with lush green plants combining to produce a unique smell and the thundering sound of a waterfall crashing down into your memories. Wandering out of the undergrowth, roul-roul

partridges wander about. Educative displays tell visitors how rubber trees are used and focus on the need for sustainability. Perhaps the best part of your visit will be the path taking you to the dizzy heights at the top of the dome, where temperatures are highest and you get to walk through the canopy of trees, gazing down on Cornwall's very own rainforest. It's a fascinating day out and one which adults will enjoy as much as the kids. But among the smiles and selfies is a very real and urgent sense of how fragile these ecosystems are. The most chilling statistic you'll leave the Eden Project with? An area of rainforest the size of this incredible biome is cut down every 11 seconds.

LEARN TO SURF IN THE SHADOW OF THE UK'S WILDEST WAVES

FISTRAL BEACH CORNWALL

Cribbar wave height 9m (30ft)

Year Cribbar was first ridden 1966

Boardmasters capacity vs population of Newquay 53,000 vs 23,000

Cornish translation of 'Cornwall' Kernow

Drive down to south-west England during the summer holiday season and you're sure to see a convoy of cars and campervans carrying surfboards heading the same way. Cornwall may not have the global surfing reputation of California the Beach Boys sang about, and it has fewer surfer dudes than eastern Australia, but the county is in a league of its own when it comes to British surfing. Not only has Kernow got the biggest waves, it's also furthest south so has the best of the summer weather as well. These two important factors combine to make it a haven for those seeking sand and surf during the school holidays.

So why does Cornwall get these monster waves that attract surfers from all over the world? Here comes the geography... Waves are created by the power of wind. Strong winds that blow far across the sea without obstacles whip it up into a frenzy, making bigger waves. Our winds blow predominantly from the south-west, and it's a long way across the Atlantic from Cornwall to South America. In a nutshell, this is why Cornish waves are quite a size.

The Cornish coast experiences oceanic swells all year round, but the winter swells are especially notorious and lead to the creation of England's biggest wave – the Cribbar. This is a frighteningly menacing reef break located at Towan Head about 1.5km (1 mile) west of the nation's surfing capital, Newquay. When the large swells hit the rocks, monstrous waves are created that take their name from the Cornish word for reef – 'kribow'. These huge waves are not to be taken lightly, though: the nickname of

the Cribbar is 'The Widowmaker'. Only those who are expert surfers should take it on. It was first ridden in 1966 by four lifeguards from Australia and the USA, who paddled out on waxless and leashless 3m (10ft) boards. While the waves in Newquay Bay can reach 2.4m (8ft) on days of good surf, the Cribbar regularly gets 9m (30ft) waves rolling in, sometimes even higher.

As we've demonstrated here, the very biggest of the Cornish waves are not to be played around with. But there's plenty of surf to have a lot of fun with on Fistral Beach, and no better place for beginners to start than at the West Country Surf School (www.surfingschool. co.uk). Even if you've got no experience of heading out onto the waves with a surfboard, the instructors at the surf school will patiently make sure you're standing up and showing off

your best Beach Boy moves in no time. My kids were experts at falling off their boards but after just an hour of tips and encouragement in a proper lesson they could stand up and successfully ride one of the waves. Most people in their group at the surf school managed it, and follow-on lessons are available for those wanting to develop their rad moves.

You can see expert surfers out on the waves at Fistral Beach most days, especially when the sun is shining and the days are long. But if you want to experience a real treat, go there during the Boardmasters Festival in August (www.boardmasters.com). As well as some of the top names in music, there are stunning surfing competitions featuring professionals from around the world. Expect the town to be inundated with young dudes and dudettes awaiting their GCSE and A Level results.

DISCOVER THE SECRETS OF THE UK'S LARGEST AQUARIUM

Marine animals
5,000+

Largest tank
2,500,000
litres (550,000
gallons)

Caribbean fish
1,000+

Opened 1998

NATIONAL MARINE AQUARIUM PLYMOUTH

There are many aquaria around the UK, but if you're wanting to explore marine biodiversity you should really head for the biggest of them all. Based in the seaside metropolis of Plymouth, the National Marine Aquarium covers all aspects of oceanic life, from the shores of Plymouth Sound to the coral reefs of eastern Australia. You'll get up close with a huge range of species, including sharks, stingrays, octopuses and jellyfish, as well as learning about the conservation work that all the profits go towards. The aquarium is not only a great day out, but it's also in a wonderful setting, right on the coast in a city with a rich seafaring history. The team here has cleverly devised an attraction that pays a great deal of attention to the coastal waters of Britain as well as bringing in the often more glamorous tropical ecosystems.

You may well have seen some of the 5,000 animals housed here before on the BBC TV show that went behind the scenes at the country's largest aquarium. *Secrets of the Aquarium* was 18 months in the making and, when broadcast, gave viewers a peek into the inner workings of the National Marine Aquarium. The film crew was given exclusive access to the work carried out by the aquarium's dedicated team, with some of the most popular moments of the six episodes focussing on specific creatures. Viewers got to know Larry the lobster as he had a new cave area constructed, followed the story of the turtle from the Maldives that needed a new home, and followed the antics of a cheeky green turtle

named Friday. It's well worth catching up with the show before you make your journey to see the aquarium in real life. That way you'll have an appreciation for the work that goes on in the background and you might even get to see some of the famous faces!

Four distinct zones demand your attention on your way around this huge aquarium. Dozens of tanks tell the story of marine life in Plymouth Sound, where there are fish and invertebrates found in the sea you can see from the shoreline, including sharks, octopuses and rays. The Eddystone Reef is found around 19km (12 miles) south of Plymouth, and the Eddystone Tank at the aquarium is all about the habitat the reef provides for marine life. There are a range of animals here that could be found in the reef environment, along with life-size models of whales and dolphins. Things

get a bit more tropical with the Atlantic zone, especially the Caribbean fish, which are housed in the largest tank in the aquarium – a real whopper containing two and a half million litres of water. You'll see sharks in this section, plus a display dedicated to the ocean's 'drifters' – jellyfish. Kids who liked *Finding Nemo* will want to see the clownfish in the Great Barrier Reef display. Importantly, as well as being a lot of fun for everyone walking around looking at the magnificent displays, there is also a lot of information about the threats being faced by the seas and oceans. Bleaching of the coral reefs and plastic pollution are just two of the main issues, and the aquarium tries hard to raise awareness.

006

RIDE THE WORLD'S STEEPEST WATER-POWERED RAILWAY

Year opened
1890

Capacity 40
people per car

Gradient
58 per cent

Length
262m (860ft)

Height
152m (499ft)

LYNTON AND LYNMOUTH CLIFF RAILWAY

In the days before cars and buses were around to power folk up steep hills with ease in a few moments, the two north Devon communities of Lynton and Lynmouth had a real divide running between them. It came in the form of a steep cliff. Perched high up, enjoying a lofty sea view, the people of Lynton could enjoy a journey down to Lynmouth, which sat next to the sea. It was the journey home they didn't relish. The 150m (492ft) cliff and the steep route between the two settlements proved to be an annoying barrier when it came to trade, tourism and even visiting friends. In the 1880s the tourist trade saw visitors arrive in Lynmouth on boats from Bristol and Swansea, but many were put off from making the trip up the steep hill to Lynton. Who can blame them? I wouldn't fancy a tiresome trek up a steep incline when the sun is beating down or there's a gale blowing in from the sea.

So, in a typically pioneering feat of Victorian engineering, Lynton and Lynmouth were linked by a railway that ensured travellers a smooth journey without breaking into a sweat. The water-powered railway was opened to the public on Easter Monday in 1890 and has been in operation ever since, transporting goods and passengers up and down the cliff and leaving only a tiny carbon footprint behind. When it was opened, this instantly became a record-breaking form of transport. It's the steepest water-powered railway in the world and also the one that climbs the highest – records it proudly still holds today.

As well as transporting people, the cars also became a game changer for tradesmen moving coal, ice, granite, petrol and cement, among other goods. Over the decades, it's been a huge boost to the local economy, proving to be a great transport asset and becoming an attraction in its own right. When you stand at the bottom of the railway and look up towards Lynton, the line disappears up the cliff at an almost impossible angle. The gradient is 58 per cent and the two cars negotiate it with a graceful glide. Try to position yourself near the front window of the car so you can make the most of the sea view but also get the opportunity to look down at the track and appreciate the astonishing angle of ascent and descent.

It's certainly a trip you will remember, definitely a unique experience. Climbing

inside the wooden carriages you can't help but raise a smile to the Victorian design, and the authenticity is enhanced by the station staff, who often dress in period uniforms. This is a record-breaking, nostalgic seaside journey you just have to take. And the ride is so smooth, it's quite incredible to think it's so old and the incline is so steep.

One other thing to bear in mind – the views are stunning. The north Devon coastline is fabulous and on a clear day you can see across to Wales. Make sure you treat yourself in a Lynton café when you're done!

007

CLIMB THE LARGEST GORGE IN ENGLAND

CHEDDAR GORGE SOMERSET

Key discovery
Cheddar Man

Cliff height
137m (450ft)

Cheddar Gorge length 4.8km (3 miles)

Created 1.2 million years ago

When in Cheddar Gorge, simply stand and gaze upwards at the immense, imposing sides of the cliff towering over you. It's a breathtaking space, formed by melting ice over a million years ago that left us with the beautiful 4.8km (3 miles) long gorge attracting thousands of tourists. It's an incredible landform, one you'll want to return to again and again. This is England's largest gorge, but the height is not the only record-breaking aspect of your visit. Within Gough Cave, one of Cheddar's most famous underground labyrinths, a significant discovery was made in 1902. It revealed the oldest skeleton ever found on these shores, a prehistoric guy now known as **Cheddar Man**.

Even to an experienced rock climber, the cliffs at Cheddar can be intimidating. They tower some 137m (450ft) above you. Before you get all your kit on, you may even have seen folks having their own rock climbing adventure and noticed how tiny they look up there! But there's no need to worry. Unless you're a pro, don't attempt to climb the cliffs by yourself, but instead sign up for one of the guided climbs on offer. Even if you have never ventured far up a climbing wall before, the guys running this activity will, ahem, show you the ropes (thank you, I'm here all week). This is a fun trip for adventurers of any ability, meaning you'll be able to tackle it at your own pace and take time to glance left and right at the amazing views – if you have a head for heights!

The beauty about the cliff climbing operation at Cheddar is that there are several different routes, each catering for different skill levels – from very easy to pretty difficult. So once you get your helmet sorted and have been given safety instructions, you'll be taken to the foot of one of their 15m (50ft) outdoor climbing walls and off you go. Seriously, what an adventure you'll have, each hand and foot hold you negotiate taking you further away from the ground and up to appreciate the peace and tranquillity of a place normally enjoyed only by the birds. The journey back down to terra firma is not as daunting as it may seem; you're lowered down gently by an instructor.

There are different experiences for adrenaline-hunting teenagers and adults, along with easier routes for adventurous kids aged over eight. And if you're a member of the British Mountaineering Council you could be able to tackle one of the 1,000 hardcore routes and enjoy unparalleled views of the surrounding landscape. Should you still be in the market for an adrenaline rush when you've ticked off all your gorge climbing goals, get your name down for the Black Cat Freefall inside Gough Cave. This chamber of the cave was named by the son of its discoverer, Richard Gough, when a light cast a shadow on the wall that looked like a black cat. Today, if you're brave enough, you can climb a 9m (30ft) ladder to the roof of the cave and make that all-important leap of faith down to the bottom. While you're at Cheddar, be sure to check out the other world-class attractions available, including the great show caves that can be toured and the subterranean light shows that will dazzle you. Activities can be booked at www. cheddargorge.co.uk.

008

NAVIGATE YOUR WAY OUT OF THE WORLD'S LONGEST MAZE

Year planted
1975

Number of yews
16,000

Area covered
1.48 acres
(6,000m^2)

Total route
2.72km (1.69 miles)

LONGLEAT SOMERSET

The Longleat Estate is no stranger to world-beating achievements. In April 1966, the 'Lions of Longleat' attraction became the first place outside Africa where wildlife fans could drive through an enclosure full of the big cats. It paved the way for the modern-day safari park, of which Longleat remains one of the best. The Longleat Estate consists of 8,000 acres (32.3km^2) that have been home to the Marquesses of Bath since 1541. As the managers of the animal attraction entered the 1970s, they were keen to create other features that would make them stand out from the other UK parks vying for tourists. One of the ideas that came to fruition was a maze. Not just any old maze but the world's longest maze. It involved planting some 16,000 English yews in a well-designed, intricate layout that created not only a fun attraction but a challenging activity that is genuinely tricky to complete. There are 2.7km (1.69 miles) of pathways twisting and turning through this phenomenal maze, which covers an area of 1.48 acres (6,000m^2).

Many dead-ends and red herrings disorientate folk brave enough to enter this huge puzzle, with the only help on hand being the six raised bridges and one central tower that allow you to gaze over the top of the hedges. But even these are limited in their assistance and, if you're anything like me, you'll be wandering around for some time, bumping into the same people over and over again, offering them advice that probably only complicates their journey and listening to tips from people who haven't the first clue where they are. It's a fun and, at times,

frustrating way to spend an afternoon that will bring the family together. Or maybe drive them all apart. Or perhaps just get them lost.

One thing is for certain: if you enter the maze you become part of this fabulous attraction's long history, where generations of children and adults have interacted with each other, sharing frustrations and solutions to achieve the joint aim of getting out. For the younger visitors, it's all about the giant hedges and the feeling of being hidden in the middle of a fairytale. Adults will also appreciate the joy of getting away from the rat race within the protection of the large, yew walls. It's like spending time on a film set or within the pages of an adventure book set in simpler times. The maze was the idea of the eccentric 7th Marquess of Bath, Alexander Thynn. He loved mazes, and as well as this world-beating effort there are other smaller

ones he had built at Longleat, including the Lunar Maze, the Sun Maze and King Arthur's Maze. Beginning with the eyebrow-raising idea to allow people to drive around lions in their cars, then moving on to the world-beating maze, innovation has long been the name of the game at Longleat.

009

Size 900 acres (3.6km²)

Crowd 210,000 people

Number of toilets 3,300

Number of bars 100

Number of food stalls 500

GLASTONBURY, SOMERSET

There are summer music festivals, and then there is Glastonbury. While other summer music line-ups try to rival the gargantuan event in Somerset, most do not come close. What started in 1970 as a pop, blues and folk festival for 1,500 people has grown into an event of mythical proportions. Today, the long weekend at Worthy Farm pulls in over 200,000 music lovers, reaches a TV audience of millions around the world and has hosted the biggest names in rock 'n' roll history. Glastonbury is simply the original and the best, the biggest greenfield music and performing arts festival on the planet.

Your first experience of this joyous festival will be to get hold of a ticket. Demand easily outstrips supply, so the application is far more complicated than for other festivals. You'll need to pre-register and keep your fingers crossed. There will be 210,000 lucky people who manage to get onto the site. Gone are the days of the 1980s and 1990s, when people were seen taking ladders in vans and using them to scale the perimeter, getting in without paying.

There was thought to be nearly 300,000 at the 1994 festival, including gatecrashers. When planning your visit, be mindful of the 'fallow years' when the countryside is allowed to recover. About every five years, the Glastonbury Festival takes a break.

Once at the event, you're sure to be overwhelmed by the sheer scale of it. This is basically a city-sized festival, with artsy folk

coming from all over the world to live and play together. There's so much variation in the line-up, you'll need to have a loose plan for what you want to see, working out when and where you want to be but accepting you'll inevitably become distracted by unexpected things you see along the way. Getting between different stages can be quite an event; the perimeter of the site is an incredible 13km (8 miles) long and, with big crowds, so you'll need to allow plenty of time for walking places. While you might have some 'must-see' acts you want to be present for, it's a good idea to leave a lot of time for random wandering about, drinking in the festival site.

This is a magical place where the best times are often unplanned; meeting new friends and getting into adventures as you discover new music. The acts booked at Glastonbury are so varied and so renowned that there is something for everyone, no matter your age or preferred genre. At other festivals you may check what the line-up of performers is before you decide to buy your weekend experience, but at Glastonbury you're pretty safe to go ahead and buy, knowing there's bound to be something special. The Glasto alumni reads like a 'Who's Who?' of music. If there's a big name out there that hasn't played on the Worthy Farm stages, it's more a question of when rather than if.

Many thousands of people who fancy experiencing Glastonbury firsthand fall at the first hurdle and don't manage to get a ticket. Fortunately, there is fabulous coverage on the BBC. Across the internet, television and radio, dozens of performances and hours of live acts are made available to those watching at home. See more at www.glastonburyfestivals.co.uk.

010

BRISTOL BALLOON FIESTA

Started 1979

Number of hot air balloons 100

Typical Daily Audience 100,000

Mass launches per day 2

There's something magical about being up close to a hot air balloon. Hearing the roar of the gas ignite, seeing the brilliantly bright flame, marvelling at the heat shimmer as the balloon inflates and witnessing the basket take the aeronaut and passengers up to the clouds. Part of the charm is its romantic link with the past. From the early versions of the Montgolfier brothers' flights, through to the famous appearance of hot air balloons in classic tales like *The Wizard of Oz* and *Around the World in 80 Days*, there is something intrinsically endearing about this form of transport. You can, of course, arrange to get in the basket and take your own flight, with several companies offering dawn and sunset voyages in our national parks. But to enjoy all things hot air balloon without forking out a fortune, there's only one place to head – Bristol.

It was in 1979 when a relatively small group of hot air balloon enthusiasts gathered together in the city and started the annual tradition. In that year, some 27 balloons were floated skywards in a mass launch, with aeronauts from the West Country being joined by others from Ireland and Germany. Fast forward to today and

interest in the Bristol Balloon Fiesta has inflated somewhat; it now lasts four days, features around 100 balloons and pulls in a crowd of half a million people.

A day at the Balloon Fiesta is a special one you are sure to remember. Get there early on your

visit because the activities kick off with the first of two mass ascents, 100 balloons filling up with hot air and heading skywards. Some stay tethered by a rope to the arena ground, while others soar over the Bristol cityscape. Along with traditional balloons, you'll see the more unusual contraptions of strange shapes and sizes; balloon spotting is truly a great family event and there have been some fabulous creations. One Bristol-made Darth Vader balloon was out of this world.

During the day, there are many different activities to take part in and lots of stalls to browse. One of the most popular things to do is chatting to the crew of the balloons, having a look at their equipment while learning about their flying experiences. In the evening, a second mass ascent takes place before what many consider to be the festival's most significant feature – the Night Glows. Here, once the summer sun sets, the balloons are lit up and a musical soundtrack adds a new dimension to a record-breaking event.

The mass ascents are not guaranteed to take place; hot air ballooning is very much dependent on the weather. Decisions on whether to fly or not are left until the last minute so that current atmospheric conditions can be taken into account. When everything goes to plan and the green light is given, it's one of the most amazing things to experience in the country.

Bristol has great form as the global centre of ballooning, and not just because of the fiesta. Only three balloons have completed a round-the-world flight and all three were made in Bristol by Cameron Balloons. Find out more at www.bristolballoonfiesta.co.uk.

RIDING THE WAVES ON BRITAIN'S LARGEST TIDAL BORE

THE RIVER SEVERN
NEWNHAM-ON-SEVERN

Wave height Up to 2m (6.6ft)

Max speed 10mph

Longest surf ride 7.6km (4.7 miles)

Number of birds wintering on the estuary 70,000

Spectators for largest bores 10,000

One of the rarest and most remarkable natural phenomena in Britain travels up the River Severn several days of the year, attracting spectators and thrill-seekers not just from this country but from around the world. The Severn Bore is a tidal event that forms when a wave surges up the estuary against the current of the river. The rising tide is funnelled into narrowing banks of the River Severn, creating a seemingly impossible wave that can reach heights of up to 2m (6.6ft) and travel at 10mph. It provides heaps of fun for experienced surfers and kayakers but is also a great event for spectators safely rooted on the bank.

Recording-breaking in more ways than one, the Severn is Britain's longest river and carries the largest volume of water. Flowing from a source way up high in the Welsh mountains, it twists and turns for 355km (220 miles) before entering the estuary. But the incredible natural feature that is the Severn bore is all about water surging upstream in a seemingly impossible turn of events. What you see when the bore hits the part of the river in front of you is simply jaw-dropping. A tall wave rolls in from the estuary, looking

like it could go on forever and giving surfers the opportunity to ride their way up the river.

Yes, you read that correctly. We're talking about surfers. On the River Severn. Heading upstream. And we're not talking about just one or two surfers, either. As the largest of the bores surge in, expect to see dozens of surfers positioned along the river waiting to catch the famous wave and ride it as long as they can. Folk in kayaks paddle ferociously to keep up with the

unusual wave. The first time you see it, it takes a while to rationalise the scene in front of you; you're just not supposed to see surfers riding a large wave up a river.

There are several opportunities to see the Severn bore every year; around 260 occur annually, on days following the new and full moon. On such days, the bores arrive with the high tide twice a day, so expect to find 130 'bore days' on the calendar. The dates and times you can witness the bore are published well in advance on several websites, including that of a pub named after the phenomenon (www. thesevernbore.com). Some months may not have any bores taking place, while others will have plenty.

The key pieces of advice for planning your Severn bore adventure are as follows: firstly,

take note of the different categories of the bore. This is based on the size of the tide and resulting height of the wave, with a 'small bore' being less than 1m (3.3ft) high and an 'exceptional bore' being over 2m (6.6ft). Secondly, scout out where you're planning on watching the bore. There are several good spotting locations, including Newnham-on-Severn, where you can gaze upon the rolling bore for several minutes. Stonebench is another great place, and the wave has been known to peak at over 2m (6.6ft) here in exceptional bores. The bore isn't a great timekeeper; sometimes it can be up to half an hour early or late, so arrive in good time. And finally, stay safe. Keep your feet firmly on the ground and don't go too near the river. The bore is potentially very dangerous and has been known to carry large items of debris up the river at high speed.

WATCH THE WORLD'S LONGEST CHEESE-ROLLING RACE

COOPER'S HILL BROCKWORTH

Number of races
4 or 5

Number of competitors
around 30

Cheese speed
Up to 70mph

Number of spectators
typically 4,000

Hill height
180m (590ft)

You've probably seen on the news the wonderfully eccentric British sport that is cheese-rolling. Every year it makes the headlines around the world simply for its bizarre nature, as competitors fall, tumble and inevitably get injured, chasing a Double Gloucester down a ridiculously steep hill in Brockworth. Several cheese-rolling competitions take place around the country but the longest course, and the one with the biggest profile, takes place on Cooper's Hill on Bank Holiday Monday at the end of May. During the day, there are typically four or five races where the participants chase a 4kg (9lb) wheel of Double Gloucester cheese down a 180m (590ft) hill with a gradient as high as 45 per cent. The whole aim is to try and grab the cheese first. Sounds simple, but it is nothing of the sort.

To see the ultimate, record-breaking cheese race, the secret is getting there early to get a good viewing spot among the thousands of people who will be alongside you. But as well as securing a place, you want to make the most of the experience. This is a magnificent community event teeming with excitement and tradition.

The cheese rolling is not just a race, but more akin to a small, eccentric, festival. There are food stalls, local sellers, tourists from all over the world, and media crews everywhere.

Once the race starts, it's both thrilling and comical to see the competitors pour over the

top of the hill chasing the giant cheese. And it's not long before people start falling, rolling and literally bouncing down the hill. There is laughter from the crowd at the sight of this, but also genuine concern. Take care. Every year there are injuries among those taking part, of course, but also among those watching who get mixed up in the action.

So just how and when did this bonkers tradition start? Wonderfully, nobody really knows. Records show it was taking place as early as the 1800s, but it's likely to have dated a lot further back in time. We may never know. But the important thing is that it's still going strong and is embraced by so many people every year.

The record-breaking winner of the cheese race on Cooper's Hill, Brockworth, is local man Chris Anderson. He has claimed the title no fewer than 23 times before announcing his cheese-rolling retirement.

There are other places around the country where you can engage in cheese rolling races and other cheese-related activities. There's the World Stilton Rolling Championships, for example, or the Chester Cheese Rolling Championships. At Ide Hill in Kent they roll Edam and in Cardiff they celebrate a cheese-tossing event. These sound like fun events, but none have the longevity and attention-grabbing power of the cheese rolling at Cooper's Hill. Just think, ahem, Caerphilly before taking part.

013

WATCH THE UK'S LARGEST DISPLAY OF TANKS IN ACTION

BOVINGTON TANK MUSEUM

Number of tanks
300

Oldest tank
1915's Little Willie

Most iconic tank
Mobile Tiger I

Chieftain tank weight
55 tonnes (121,254lbs)

Having had a huge influence on warfare for over a century and swayed the outcome of many a conflict, the tank is one of the most intimidating and terrifying vehicles ever made. Though you certainly wouldn't want to come face to face with one in a dark alley, there is an eerie satisfaction in getting up close to something so dangerous you usually only see in the movies. The place for that is undoubtedly the Tank Museum at Bovington, where you'll see not only the largest assembly of tanks on display in the country, but also rarities like the only running German Tiger I. There are nine exhibitions where you'll learn about the history of tank warfare and discover stories about specific models, including Whippet, Panther, Chieftain and Little Willie.

Today, Little Willie is a curious name for something so ferocious, but it actually came from the German Crown Prince, Kaiser Wilhelm, and his childhood nickname. Combining armoured protection with a combustion engine and tracks, Little Willie was the world's first working tank and the trailblazer for all future tanks. But its duty life was short-lived. The innovative idea making Little Willie so special was the tracks allowing it to travel across battlefields, but this was swiftly improved upon. Tanks were soon given bigger tracks so they could tackle trenches. Little Willie was pretty much retired as soon as it was built.

Fast forward to World War II and the armoured tank was a much more complex and formidable beast. The German Tiger I is the most recognisable of all the 1940s tanks and the only running version is found here at the museum. This one was captured in Tunisia on April 24th 1943 and you can see it in action at the annual Tiger Day event. It's a very nippy and versatile tank, but its armour at the front was 10cm (3.9in) thick and resistant to Allied guns. Its own gun could penetrate similar armour at a range of 1,000m (3,280ft). No wonder it filled the Allies with so much dread.

Britain's main tank for twenty years was the Chieftain, a vehicle that boosted the nation's deterrence during the Cold War. The tank's engine was designed by Leyland and based on a pre-war German aircraft. It used diesel and had six forward speeds as well as a reverse.

There were 4,400 Chieftain tanks produced during the uncertain years of the 1960s, 1970s and 1980s, and they included some brand new design features. For example, the driver's seat allowed the tank to be smaller; the driver lies in a reclined position and changes the gear with their foot.

The pinnacle of the tank fan's calendar has to be TANKFEST weekend, which takes place over three days of explosive action in and around the museum's arena. During this summer spectacular, visitors get the chance to see a wide range of different tanks in mock-combat scenarios, engage with history reenactment camps, and attend lectures by military experts. To book onto this fiery weekend and take a stroll around a record-breaking world of tanks, visit www.tankmuseum.org.

WATCH A MOVIE IN THE UK'S SMALLEST CINEMA

Number of screens 3

Total number of seats 27

Screen width 3m (10ft)

Opened 2013

BOURNEMOUTH COLOSSEUM

There are so many options available now when you're booking cinema tickets, it can become a bit overwhelming. Do you want to see the film in standard 2D? Is an average size screen OK or should you indulge in an iMax experience? How about 4DX? Do you need to feel the special effects hit you full in the face like you're part of the action? What about your seats? Should they be VIP or bog standard? Reclining? Sofa? And would you like popcorn, nachos, hot dogs, cocktails or an all-you-can-eat restaurant extravaganza as you watch the plot unfold?

Sometimes, it's better to cut out the fuss and go for the simpler option. Just sit back and enjoy the narrative. This is certainly what you get when you book tickets to see a film at what is officially the UK's smallest cinema. You'll find the Bournemouth Colosseum beneath a café in the town's Westbourne Arcade. To be fair, the name 'Colosseum' might be a bit of a stretch. Such a grand name implying a venue on a large scale is more than a little tongue in cheek.

Although this is a cinema with three screens, it's as far removed from a multiplex as it's possible to get. There are just 27 seats available. And that's across all screens.

Carpeted and with movie memorabilia on the walls, the theatre spaces at the Colosseum are homely and welcoming. It's more like watching a film in a lavish front room, and as a result it's a much more personal, welcoming experience

than you might get at an out-of-town complex sweeping thousands of people into 20 screens along a constantly moving conveyor belt. It's the intimacy that has people raving about it on review websites. Get enough people together and you can fill this place with friends and family, having the whole cinema to yourself for a private screening. The Colosseum is very much a place where you can hang out, have something to eat, enjoy a drink and then relax watching a classic film, or maybe an art house production.

Cult films also get shown here, but what you won't find are the big-budget, mainstream releases at the same time they're shown elsewhere. The Colosseum prides itself on having a specialist, carefully-thought-out programme of features and doesn't attempt to compete with the big chains. You'll come across a diverse listing of movies, some of them decades old. But one thing's for sure; when the credits roll at the end of your picture, you'll have enjoyed a unique cinematic experience you'll never forget. And next time you head to see a blockbuster at the retail park multiplex, there may well be a part of you that misses the calm and intimacy that the Bournemouth Colosseum has to offer. Have a look at what's available when you visit at www. bournemouthcolosseum.com.

015

SPEND AN AFTERNOON EXPLORING BRITAIN'S LONGEST BEACH

CHESIL BEACH
JURASSIC COAST

Length 29km (18 miles)

Width up to 200m (655ft)

Number of annual visitors 500,000

Estimated number of pebbles 180 billion

Ready for a day at Britain's longest beach? No need to pack your bucket and spade, though. And I'm not sure those shorts will be needed either. Welcome to Chesil Beach on the south coast of England, a pebbly delight stretching out as far as the eye can see and experiencing frequently chilly winds blown in from the sea. This may not be your typical 'sandcastles and ice creams' idea of a day out at the seaside, but this is one of the most unique coastal landforms on the planet and, as such, makes a magnificent place to explore. You'll find Chesil Beach on the world-famous Jurassic Coast; along with a string of other significant landforms, this shingle stretch is part of a UNESCO World Heritage Site.

A walk on Chesil Beach is a rewarding experience and can last pretty much as long as you'd like it to. The pebble surface makes for a more difficult stroll than a sandy beach, and the sheer length of this natural feature means you're unlikely to make much of an inroad into it during a morning or afternoon. But you can plan a 'there and back' adventure to fit in with your own timescale. What you're walking on (also probably slipping and falling on) is a tombolo. Not one of the games at a school summer fayre where you pull out raffle tickets and hope to win a bottle of half-used shower gel. That's a tombola. A tombolo is a geographical term for a narrow beach that connects an island to the mainland. The island, in this case, is Portland, which sits just off Weymouth. Chesil Beach runs in a long, 29km

(18 miles) line, starting from West Bay and eventually linking up with Portland.

As every GCSE geographer worth their salt will tell you, this unusual landform is created by the process of longshore drift, where waves slowly but surely move material along the coast. As you walk along the tombolo you'll see the size of the pebbles gradually change; on the eastern end near Portland they are large and rounded, becoming smaller and more angular as you head west because the sea can easily carry the smaller material further. There are few better opportunities in the UK to wander through a wonder of physical geography. Better bring some sturdy footwear, though, because this is not a place for flip flops. If you're not into walking, there are other activities making Chesil Beach a must-visit destination. Swimming is not advised at all because of the dangerous

currents, but fishing is popular, and there are kayakers who like to head out into the lagoon.

As you'll come to appreciate when you explore Chesil Beach, the sea breaks on the southern shore of the tombolo, while to the north there are lagoons, saltmarshes and mudflats separating it from the mainland. This is a place where wildlife can thrive, and you'll not be surprised to learn this whole area is a Site of Special Scientific Interest. There are hundreds of bird species and plenty of swans in the lagoon. It is home to many species of fish, molluscs and crustaceans, including the starlet sea anemone and the lagoon sand shrimp.

016

ENJOY THE ATTRACTIONS AT BRITAIN'S OLDEST THEME PARK

Opened
1843

Size 40 acres
(0.16km²)

**Number of
annual visitors**
150,000

**Number of
attractions**
40+

BLACKGANG CHINE
ISLE OF WIGHT

Plenty of theme parks are now well established in the UK and have been around for decades. But the oldest one on our shores? It's been around since the 19th century, and to experience the charms it offers you'll need to get yourself down to the fabulous holiday destination that is the Isle of Wight. Blackgang Chine has been visited by millions of people over the years, and there's a mix of big rides and cute family attractions for all to enjoy.

It's true that the Isle of Wight is a very popular place for people to spend their holidays, but many tourists taking the ferry across the Solent from Portsmouth will be surprised to learn it's been home to a theme park for so long. So just how did Blackgang Chine get established in the Victorian era here so far from the big city populations? And what on earth is the name about? Well, it all started with an entrepreneur called Alexander Dabell, who wanted to dabble in the entertainment business. On a visit to the site, he saw the potential of the chine, a

large coastal gorge, and realised he could plant gardens and create attractive paths down to it. He acquired the land in an unusual way by today's standards: he threw a stone as far as he could, on the understanding that he could lease the land up to where the stone landed.

And so it was that Dabell assembled a range of attractions appealing to inquisitive Victorian travellers who were into exploring new places, thanks to rail links, and were obsessed with 'healthy' destinations. Blackgang Chine, then,

was opened as a park of curiosities in 1843. One of the initial points of interest of this long-lasting attraction was the skeleton of a whale that had caused quite a stir when it washed up near The Needles in 1842. Dabell won the whale in an auction, sold off the blubber and bleached the bones before transporting them to the park. Although the chine has disappeared, a sorry victim of coastal erosion, the whale bones are still in place, a reminder of the park's origins.

Blackgang Chine markets itself as the country's oldest theme park, but you shouldn't go along expecting a day out that's comparable to Thorpe Park or Alton Towers. This is a totally different experience. There are fewer white knuckles found here and more holding hands looking at family-friendly exhibits. Good rides are still here, though, and some of them are fairly extreme, spinning you through 360° and leaving your stomach behind on a vertical drop. The thrill-seeking rides here go by the names of Extinction, Evolution and Shipwrecked, and one of the latest additions, the Jolly Robin spooky ship. If spooky things and ghosts are your thing, you've come to the right place. People of a nervous disposition should probably know (or perhaps shouldn't be told) that Blackgang Chine is reportedly one of the most haunted places in Britain.

Some have preferred to call Blackgang Chine an 'amusement park', but I guess it doesn't really matter about a subtle difference in words. The bottom line is this: when it comes to paying admission to a park rammed with different attractions, Blackgang Chine was a trailblazer and is still around today for you to explore. Plan your trip at www.blackgangchine.com.

Castle grounds
13 acres
(52,609km²)

**Biggest number
of guests for a
state banquet**
162

**Water used in
1992** 6.8 million
litres (1.5 million
gallons)

**Number of
kitchen staff**
33

MARVEL AT THE WORLD'S OLDEST AND BIGGEST INHABITED CASTLE

WINDSOR CASTLE

Built on the order of William the Conqueror in 1070, and completed by 1086, no castle in the world comes close to the grandeur, importance and historical significance of the one standing at Windsor. It has stood proud and watched the nation develop and change over the last millennia. As you might imagine, of a building that has witnessed the history of our nation since the Norman Conquest, Windsor Castle makes for one cracking day for anybody with half an interest in the past.

The key events this castle has been a part of would fill any school history textbook with drama and intrigue. The Order of the Garter was created here. It was used as the headquarters for Oliver Cromwell, who also used it to imprison Charles I and his Royalists. It's played host to a huge number of foreign dignitaries, including American presidents, world leaders and members of royal families. Napoleon and Tsar Nicholas II are but two of the big historical names. Queen Elizabeth II spent a

lot of time here, and now it's one of the official residences of King Charles III. Many monarchs are buried in the fabulously gothic St George's Chapel, including Queen Elizabeth II, and it has hosted several royal weddings, most recently Prince Harry's marriage to Meghan Markle.

Windsor is very much on the established tourist trail for foreign visitors wanting an essential taste of Britain. Within easy reach of London for a day trip, coach loads of visitors

turn up here daily and join the many domestic sightseers wanting to see the inside of this world-famous building. There's a wealth of important rooms and buildings to explore once you're on the inside of the castle walls, meaning a trip to Windsor can easily take up a full day – and be as tiring as it is exciting. One of the highlights of your trip around the castle is the State Apartments, which have been used many times down the years to entertain leaders from a host of other countries. Keep an eye out for a large malachite urn that was presented to Queen Victoria by Tsar Nicholas I in 1839. Picture the grand dances and meals that have taken place here.

A little harder to imagine among all the elaborate decoration and furniture is the extensive fire damage that hit this room during the 1992 blaze. Another feature that has many

visitors pointing, gasping and reaching for their camera is the Doll's House built in the early 1920s for Queen Mary. Using the term 'Doll's House' does not do this masterpiece of toy creation any justice, really. This is a miniature house within a house like you've never seen before. The attention to detail is staggering. No fewer than 1,500 of the finest artists, craftspeople and manufacturers contributed to the magnificent house at the beginning of the 20th century. Take your time looking at the many components of each room, from the wine cellar and saloon to the dining room and garden. The house even has electricity and running water.

Try to be at the castle in good time for Changing the Guard, which takes place every day at 11am. For more information, take a look at www.rct.uk/visit/windsor-castle.

TAKE GIANT STRIDES THROUGH THE WORLD'S OLDEST MODEL VILLAGE

BEKONSCOT MODEL VILLAGE

Number of buildings 200

Number of tiny inhabitants 3,000

Number of tiny animals 1,000

Number of passenger trains 10

Length of track 450m (1,500ft)

Navigating your way around a model village, gazing at tiny cricketers and little children on a miniature carousel, feels like a particularly British eccentricity. You may have visited one when you were younger, or you may now have young people in the family who have yet to make their first visit to one of these remarkable, make-believe lands. Trips to model villages are nostalgic journeys back in time, both because they may bring back happy childhood memories and also because the models themselves portray a simpler time in the past. If you're going to get involved in a model village trip, you may as well start with a record-breaker. Bekonscot Model Village is the oldest you can see in the world, on land covering 1.5 acres (6,070m²) and has one of the largest model railways in the UK running through it.

The world is literally at your feet as you wander around Bekonscot Model Village, as the kingdom of the little folk goes on beneath you. The model village is actually made up of seven different settlements, each with their own quirky features. The first is Greenhaily, a lovely community with a large zoo containing 75-year-old animals made from limewood by children in the New Forest. In Hanton, a wedding is taking place on the hill and the longest-running roadworks in Britain can be found – this route was closed in 1983 and the work still isn't finished! The fishing village of Southpool is home to rock climbers and an oil refinery, while Bekonscot town has a lifeboat station and the world's smallest M&S. Epwood

is an old mining village, with nearby Splashyng being a little more twee with its racecourse and Morris dancers.

And the New Town opened in 2018. This is a more modern affair, with a cinema and underground railway. Linking all these places, criss-crossing across the whole attraction, is the stunning model railway. Passenger and freight trains are busy at work in this meticulously designed 1:32 scale recreation started in 1929 and continuously updated ever since. The level of detail involved in this railway – and indeed everywhere throughout the model village – is quite simply stunning, even down to mosses and lichen on the rocks at the side of the line. For a glimpse into this world before you visit, head to their website (www.bekonscot.co.uk) and check out the 'Driver's eye view' video. You get lost in the footage, believing it to be a video taken in a

real train until you see somebody's gigantic legs standing on a bridge above the track.

Before you head home, experience the model village from a different perspective by visiting High Shrunkham Junction. Stepping inside the waiting room you shrink down to see what it's like for the scaled down miniature people around the Bekonscot. Look through the large window and you'll see huge humans gazing in, pointing and laughing at your diddy demeanour. When you leave the waiting room you are your normal size again, which is fortunate or you could have had a real problem driving home.

There are over 3,000 plants and trees that play a vital role in the appearance of the village, perfectly maintained by a team of gardeners to ensure they fit in with the buildings and also appear like they are to scale.

019

Top speed
81mph

Height 71.9m
(235.9ft)

**Number of
inversions** 2

Cost of build
£18 million

BE THRILLED BY BRITAIN'S FASTEST COASTER

HYPERIA THORPE PARK

When it comes to roller coaster speed, Thorpe Park has definitely edged in front of other British theme parks. The Surrey attraction boasts not just the fastest in the UK, but also the second fastest. For several years, the record-breaker was Stealth – a fast accelerator that takes you to dizzying heights. In 2024, however, Hyperia was opened and with it came the promise that it would go a whole 1mph faster. The boundaries were pushed, the record was broken, and Thorpe Park remains the Queen of Speed. It's not just the fastest, it's also the tallest, capturing the record from The Big One at Blackpool. The name comes from the type of the ride, a hypercoaster, but was also inspired by an ancient Greek goddess. A hypercoaster is a ride that has a drop of at least 61m (200ft), as this does, while Hyperia was a fearless goddess born to the river god Inachus.

With crazy stats and an impressive legend to boot, the stage was set for the birth of an iconic UK ride. Hyperia begins with a lengthy climb as your carriage is pulled up on a chain, as so many roller coasters are, though not normally to these heights. And then the release and the mega drop that leaves your stomach in the sky

before hitting you with a couple of stunningly fast inversions. When it's over, you're left in no doubt that you've been on one of the best roller coasters in the world.

But why go on the fastest ride without tackling the second fastest too? On Stealth, you'll be

propelled forward from 0 to 80mph in just two seconds. This ride has the brake horsepower of, not one, but two Formula 1 racing cars. Sat in pairs in a drag car coaster carriage, the first sign of your imminent departure comes when you see the red traffic lights above your head. There are five of them and, one by one, they turn on. When all five red lights are lit and your anxiety reaches fever pitch, the lights suddenly switch to green. These lights linger above your head for merely a moment, but it's long enough to instill a mixture of fear and excitement before the ride begins and you're careering ahead in two seconds of insane acceleration.

Almost immediately, the climb begins. Rising extremely quickly to a height just shy of 72m, you're on the tallest ride in the UK. And then the huge drop follows, emphasising just how high you have been rocketed. During this

incredibly powerful rise and fall, your body will experience a G-Force of 4.5G. It's quite something, and it's not for the faint-hearted.

Thorpe Park was developed as a theme park during the 1980s and built on land previously used by a concrete company. Its first roller coaster opened in 1984 and the park continued to grow into the huge visitor attraction it is today. Don't think that it's is all about white knuckle rides and high-speed records, though. There are plenty of rides here to keep all the family entertained for at least a couple of days. Try out Ghost Train, Tidal Wave and Colossus. Adult visitors would do well to try out their nerves on Saw: The Ride and The Walking Dead: The Ride. It's a fabulous day out, but don't say you haven't been warned!

020

ENJOY A GLASS OR TWO AT THE LARGEST VINEYARD IN THE UK

DENBIES WINE ESTATE

Size of vineyard
265 acres
(1.1km²)

Number of annual visitors
450,000

Yield
300,000 litres
(65,990 gallons)
of wine

Percentage of wine sold on site
65 per cent

It's time to treat yourself. Plan a trip to the Denbies Estate in the North Downs, where some 265 acres (1.107km²) of chalky land support the largest vineyard in the UK, and sample the delightful fruits of this huge grape-growing operation. By French or Californian standards this kind of grape-growing area is not so huge, it has to be said. But compared to other outfits in the UK at our northern latitude, this is a ginormous area. Wine being the popular drink that it is and intrigue about English wine being high, this vineyard attracts around 450,000 visitors a year, many of whom will enjoy a sample of the wine and give an approving nod to the standard of the beverage produced here.

At the heart of the visitor experience is the indoor wine tasting, which begins with a short film in the cinema. It's about the vineyard through the seasons, showing how the estate is managed come rain, sun or snow. And yes, the scenes of the vineyard covered in snow will make you realise the challenges of producing wine with the UK's climate. The snowy scenes are a long way from the sun swept hills of the south of France. It's a good introduction to the history of the vineyard and the estate in general, explaining how factors such as the geology and climate are important. You'll have a fuller picture of the overall process of English wine-making, from the vine to the bottle.

Your visit isn't all going to take place indoors, though. The vineyard is out there in the sunshine (hopefully) so take advantage of the opportunity and have a journey around the estate. On a good day, the views are exquisite, and you might actually feel like you're in France. The vineyard tour takes 50 minutes and you're driven around the extensive grounds in a train-like carriage. All the while you'll be listening to a recorded commentary about the grapes in front of you and the immense amount of work that goes on looking after them. The setting is stunning, panoramic vistas of the North Downs opening up at every turn. And no matter what time of year you visit, you'll be at a special stage in the annual circle of vineyard life. Whether it's the first buds opening up in spring or the grape-filled vines of late summer and autumn, you'll need your camera whatever the season.

You can make a day of it by visiting some of the businesses located within the estate, each offering something special to enhance your visit. Relax with a coffee, visit to the brewery, or make a therapeutic call at the spa. Or, if you're feeling energetic, you can hire a bike and take a tour of the local environs. One thing you will want to do before you leave is sample some of the Denbies Estate wine and perhaps invest in a bottle or two to take along with you. Just make sure you've got a designated driver or a taxi on hand. This record-breaking vineyard has got its unique visitor experience well-polished, meaning you are sure to have a memorable day out. Plan your day at www.denbies.co.uk.

021

TAKE A SWIM IN THE UK'S LARGEST LIDO

Surface area
91.4m x 30.2m
(100yds x 33yds)

Opened 1906

Volume of water
3.8 million litres
(1 million gallons)

TOOTING BEC LIDO

Taking a dip in chilly fresh water and going for a swim beneath an open sky has become an increasingly popular pastime. Stepping into cold water may have been seen as a crazy thing to do a few years ago, but more and more people are becoming fans of this quirky outdoor activity. Experts advise outdoor swimmers to go to organised, official venues rather than potentially dangerous spots in rivers and reservoirs.

And so, to keep safe and tick off yet another record-breaking British activity, why not make a splash at the biggest outdoor freshwater pool we have to offer? That's what you'll find at Tooting Bec Lido, South-West London, where this refreshing and energising body of water is waiting for you. The lido is one of the oldest outdoor pools in the country, opened in 1906 and measuring 100 yards by 33 yards, or 91.4m x 30.2m in today's money. You'll find the lido on Tooting Bec Common, where it was originally built with an earth ramp surrounding it so people

taking the waters could not be looked upon by folk walking on the common.

The idea for the leading lido came from a local Reverend, John Anderson. As well as providing benefits to the local population, it was his belief that the digging of the pool would provide much-needed work for local men who were out of work. And so it became one of the many outdoor swimming pools – later named lidos – that opened up across Britain at that time. Thankfully, it's one of the few that managed to survive without being closed down. But

although this outdoor pool is over 100 years old, the facilities here are modern and you'll be well-catered for. The changing cubicles running alongside the pool are well-known for being painted alternating bright red, yellow and green. Several adverts have been filmed in front of these famous changing rooms, but their most iconic appearance came in the movie Snatch during Brad Pitt's boxing scene.

The pool is open during the spring and summer months (check times at www.placesleisure.org/centres/tooting-bec-lido) but you may want to check the weather before setting out. There's a big difference in the tolerance levels needed for a visit to the lido on a hot afternoon or an early morning swim where the thermometer is hovering around the 5°C mark. If you're a bit nesh, waiting for warm weather is advisable. Even then, some may find it a bit of a challenge

immersing themselves in water that isn't heated. The secret is to count to three and duck down swiftly so your shoulders are covered. Probably. Before you know it, your body will have acclimatised and you'll soon find it more comfortable in the water than out of it.

If it is your first time for an outdoor dip, there are few places better to begin than in Tooting Bec Lido. The chances are you will become a firm fan. And if you're living nearby, you can always invest in an annual membership and go along as many times as you like.

022

Opened 1759

Size 300 acres (1.2km²)

Number of annual visitors 1.35 million

Height of titan arum 3m (9.8ft)

What it smells of dead stuff

TITAN ARUM KEW GARDENS

It's quite rare for a plant to become a major tourist attraction, but crowds certainly flock to see the titan arum at Kew Gardens – especially on the rare occasions when it's in flower. What makes it so remarkable that visitors are willing to get up close to this giant flora is that it quite literally stinks.

The world's smelliest plant is also known as the 'corpse flower,' a charming name reflecting how it stinks like dead animals. Some flowers lure pollinators with a floral bouquet, but titan arum draws in those who love to feed on rotting flesh. Even the interior colour of the flower – a dark burgundy – has the appearance of decaying flesh bodies. This is a plant that has survived because it is great at impersonating a corpse.

And so to the records. As well as being the smelliest, the titan arum has the largest unbranched inflorescence in the world. An inflorescence is a flower structure containing smaller flowers within it, just in case you wondered. It can stand as high as 3m (9.8ft) tall and contains both male and female flowers. To avoid self-pollination, the female flower opens first, stays open for a couple of days, then the male takes over. While the female is in bloom, the malevolent odour is transmitted up to half a mile away, drawing in insects that deposit pollen. When the male flower opens, it covers the insects in pollen and they eventually fly off to deposit it in another, nearby female flower. Pollinated flowers then produce bright red and orange fruits. In a year when the titan arum does not flower, it instead produces a leaf that

grows to be up to 6m (20ft) high – the largest in the world.

This highly unusual plant is endemic to the island of Sumatra in Indonesia. It grows there on the limestone hills in the rainforest. The first flowering of the plant outside of its native home happened right here at Kew in 1889. Researchers at Bonn University were instrumental in creating conditions in which the plant could survive and thrive. Sadly, the destruction of the Indonesian rainforest is drastically affecting the number of titan arum growing there, putting it under severe threat and making the conservation work at Kew all the more important.

There's so much to see and do at Kew Gardens that you can easily fill a day in what is recognised as the most biodiverse place on the planet. This is a UNESCO World Heritage Site and contains over 50,000 plant species within it. Some of the rarest and most threatened species find a space to thrive in Temperate House, the world's largest Victorian glasshouse. And the Princess of Wales Conservatory is the place to investigate to see whether the world's smelliest plant is in bloom. Check out information before you go at www.kew.org.

023

Length of course
300m (984ft)

Descent 5m
(16ft)

**GB medal haul
at the 2012
Olympics**
gold and silver in
the canoe slalom

**Chance of
ending in the
water** high

LEE VALLEY WHITE WATER CENTRE LONDON

I've been white-water rafting before on fast-flowing rivers in Iceland and Canada, but I've never been asked to do a 'swim test' before entering the boat. To qualify for this watery activity, you first don a reassuringly warm wetsuit and all-important life jacket, then jump into the rapids and float feet-first down the course to get safely to the side. Once the session starts it's simply thrilling from start to finish. Navigating around this Olympic course several times, each circuit starts with the boat climbing up a conveyor belt to gain height and then you're at the mercy of the water. You're also at the mercy of your guides, all of whom seemed excellent at gauging the right mix of excitement, adrenaline and reassurance for their passengers. The guides know where the hottest white-water action is on the course and by instructing their team to carry out simple actions they are able to build the severity of the experience up over the session.

It starts out pretty tame as you learn to row at various speeds when told to, lean over to the left or right when the order comes, and crouch down for protection when the going gets really tough. And by the last circuit, the going did get tough, but in my case the tough didn't get going – they got thrown out of the vessel into a rapid so rough it would have looked at home as a CGI effect in Pirates of the Caribbean. We were asked if we were up for it and to be fair we all said, 'yes' despite being able to see people on the boat in front of us being flung into the water as if the kraken was attacking the boat.

And so we bravely went forth, steering into one of the strongest rapids and feeling ourselves tip up at a tighter and tighter angle. For a split second it seemed like we were in control. But then, despite holding on for dear life, I was the first to be ejected and found myself under water. When I popped up above the surface, I saw the boat had completely flipped over and everybody had ended up in the rapids. Some people were already quite a way downstream, carried along by the current. Ropes were thrown in swiftly to help people get to shore in a well-managed recovery and everybody emerged safely, with huge smiles on their faces after they got their thoughts together and realised the extent of their watery adventure.

This was unlike any other white-water rafting experience. It was more extreme, but also more managed. And because it was going around the same circuit, it avoided the necessity of bus rides back to the start as you have to do in the wild. Walking back to the changing rooms after this fabulous experience, it was obvious why you had to pass the 'swim test' at the start; they wanted you ready for extreme events. White-water rafting is available in other places across the UK, and after heavy rain the rivers may indeed run wild. But for a guaranteed buzz, for a definite rush of adrenaline, following the route of triumphant Olympians is a phenomenal way to enjoy some of the toughest rapids in safe and secure conditions. Explore the range of activities available at the Lee Valley Water Centre at www.visitleevalley.org.uk.

024

CYCLE ON THE UK'S ONLY OLYMPIC INDOOR TRACK

LEE VALLEY VELO PARK LONDON

Nickname
The Pringle

Track material
Siberian pine

Number of nails used 300,000

Track length
250m (820ft)

Likely emotions
fear and excitement

I never had a bicycle as a kid but fast forward a few decades and I'm a keen cyclist who heads out on two wheels every day the weather permits. The catalyst for this transformation was twofold. The UK hosting the first stages of the Tour de France back in 2014 was a key influence, as was the success of Team GB in the 2012 London Olympics. Seeing athletes like Sir Chris Hoy and Dame Sarah Storey bomb around the beautiful Velodrome, competing in a series of events with increasingly complicated rules, was something that got the heart racing. It's a testimony to the legacy of the London Olympics that cycling fans can now book in and have a go at racing around the track where so many GB gold medals were won.

The good thing is you don't need to worry about having kit worth thousands of pounds. I'm not a fan of dressing up in Lycra like a cosplay Olympian and was pleased to see I didn't look out of place in my t-shirt and shorts. Your trainers will be fine, and you don't need to bring a helmet or bike because they're provided for you. Before you know it, you're on the floor in the middle of the famous Velodrome receiving a safety briefing before you start building up to your fastest lap. The safety talk basically came down to a couple of top tips – keep pedalling and don't steer. The Velodrome track is much steeper than I imagined. It's not quite 'Wall of Death' territory, but it's the same principle and there's a risk of falling off if you're too slow on the slope. The curved track, we're told, will guide us around the corners, so no need to turn into

them; just keep your acceleration as high as you're comfortable with.

It's easier said than done. The first few laps, strapped into the pedals and getting to grips with not having any brakes, were tough. The track is deceptively steep and the corners really do need a high speed to enter or you end up drifting down into the safety of the blue lane that's intended for slowing down. There's a black lane on the track that represents the shortest distance around the circuit. To overtake, you need to divert up the slope. Not that I managed to overtake all that much. Mainly, people were zipping by me; it really took some getting used to. But then everything seemed to slip into place and I suddenly found myself getting confident, picking up speed and moving higher on the track to drop onto the start line with extra

pace. The whole group was getting better with each lap.

But it's the last lap that matters. That's the one that's the timed one. It's all been building up to this. And just to make sure everybody knows how well – or not – you perform, your name is now put on the scoreboard as your lap is recorded with top tech. Once around you go to build up speed, sticking as close as you can to that all-important black line, and then the bell goes and you pedal like you've never pedalled before. I thought I did really well, but the scoreboard told a different story. No matter, I still got a certificate to say I'd completed a super lap at the Velodrome and nobody can take that away. What a thrilling experience it was to step into the ultimate cycling arena, work up a sweat and go home with a world-beating sense of achievement.

025

WHIZZ DOWN THE WORLD'S TALLEST AND LONGEST TUNNEL SLIDE

ARCELORMITTAL ORBIT LONDON

Number of bolts used 35,000

Slide height 76m (249ft)

Slide length 178m (584ft)

Speed 15mph

Number of steps 455

The ArcelorMittal Orbit, a stone's throw away from the Olympic Stadium, awaits you for a super slippery adventure. Some of Britain's most memorable sporting moments took place close to this iconic structure during the glorious Olympic summer of 2012 One phenomenal day became known as 'Super Saturday', when British athletes Jessica Ennis, Mo Farah and Greg Rutherford all won gold medals within a remarkable 45-minute period. It all happened in front of 80,000 bedazzled fans at the purpose-built stadium which now hosts West Ham United FC's home games.

Overseeing all this hope and achievement, the ArcelorMittal Orbit is an eye-catching, looping tower and observation point offering 20-mile (32.1km) views over Queen Elizabeth Olympic Park and out over the capital city's skyline. It has stood here as gold medals were given out, as the opening and closing ceremonies bookended the games, and as thousands of fans cheered along the twists and turns of the Premier League. Today, the iconic red Orbit

offers you the chance to get involved in a record-breaking activity because this is now officially the world's longest tunnel slide, run by adventure company ZipWorld.

Containing enough steel to make 265 double-decker London buses and held together by an incredible 35,000 bolts, the ArcelorMittal Orbit pulled in 130,000 visitors during the Olympic Games. Back then, it was already

an incredible structure, but it has proved popular among fun-seekers since having the tunnel slide added in 2016. Steel was chosen as a building material because of its recyclable nature, and indeed 60 per cent of this structure has been recycled from other products such as washing machines and cars.

Booking ahead (at www.zipworld.co.uk) is advised, especially in school holidays and at weekends. You'll choose a time slot and when you arrive the first thing to do is stand at the bottom of the structure and simply gaze up. The 600 prefabricated nodes twist and turn to form this mesmerising superstructure. The frame was constructed first, with the lift and viewing platform added after. And it's the viewing platform where you head first, ascending quickly in the lift and taking in the skyline of London on the way. You might want

to think about what time to head to the top for your slide down; dusk is my favourite as you get to see the sunset, the light fade away and the lights start to turn on.

Enjoy this beautiful view of the capital city as you explore the viewing platform, but sooner or later you're going to have to make the decision to leave. And just like in Enid Blyton's Faraway Tree, there's a much easier and more thrilling way to get down. It's slide time!

The world's tallest and longest tunnel slide is not for the faint-hearted; it's fast and there are many twists and turns. The outer edge of the slide is transparent so you can see the ground approaching as you slide through the air; not something everybody may appreciate and more than a few sliders end up closing their eyes in a roller coaster fashion.

026

Height 135m
(443ft)

**Number of
capsules** 32

Diameter
120m (393ft)

Cost of build
£70 million

Top speed
0.6mph

TAKE A TRIP AROUND THE WORLD'S LARGEST CANTILEVERED OBSERVATION WHEEL

LONDON EYE

When the London Eye was officially opened by Prime Minister Tony Blair as the 21st century loomed large on New Year's Eve, 1999, it was the largest Ferris wheel in the world. Initially known as the 'Millennium Wheel' and part of London's celebrations to welcome in the year 2000, it was supposed to be a temporary fixture on the city's skyline. Approved to stay in place for just five years, the popularity of the wheel was such that it has become one of the capital's most popular attractions among both foreign and domestic tourists. Since the London Eye was hoisted into place, a colossal wheel in Las Vegas has taken the top spot as the world's biggest, but the Eye remains the UK's biggest Ferris wheel. And, because it is suspended on only one side, it remains the largest cantilever wheel in the world.

Although it might be fun to experience a central London big wheel that spins round at a fair pace, this is not what the London Eye is about. It's a slow, steady, graceful affair. And while you may at first feel short-changed at only completing one full circle, you're given plenty of time to enjoy the far-reaching views. Almost as soon as the journey begins, you gain enough height to start gazing, chatting and

pointing out recognisable buildings. You gain a better vantage point with each second you climb and very quickly you'll be high above London's bustling streets and busy river. Clever engineering means your capsule always stays poking out from the main wheel and yet, when you're inside, it appears not to move and you obviously stay upright for the whole journey. It's easy to take this mechanical mastery for

granted but you should spare a thought for how this happens when you're in one of the 32 capsules. Note that the capsules are numbered 1–33; however, nobody really wants a ride in capsule 13, do they?

This isn't an experience that gets old or tiresome. I've been full circle on the London Eye several times now and each journey around has been fun. Gazing out at the famous skyline from this unique angle just doesn't grow old. There are so many exciting, nationally important things to make out. From Trafalgar Square to Buckingham Palace, from St Paul's Cathedral to the Shard. Information boards and occasional commentary help you identify those iconic sights.

It's important to think about when you want to start your London Eye journey. Do you want to see the capital's skyline at night with all the neon lights or during the day so you can better pick out key landmarks? Or maybe at dusk to see the sunset and sky's changing colours. Your trip does need booking in advance, but if you can check the long-term weather forecast before you fork out for it you may do yourself a favour. The last thing you want is a foggy day when you can't make much out. There's more than one kind of ticket; you can pay extra to beat the queues and get fast-tracked to the front if you're in a rush or just don't fancy standing in line. There are also super posh champagne options if you're heading to this record-breaker for a special occasion.

027

Number of steps to top 394

Big Ben weight 13 tonnes (28,660lbs)

Elizabeth Tower height 96m (315ft)

Size of gap between minute markers 30cm (12 inches)

STAND INSIDE THE WORLD'S BIGGEST AND MOST FAMOUS FOUR-FACED CHIMING CLOCK

QUEEN ELIZABETH TOWER LONDON

As buildings go, Queen Elizabeth Tower is probably the most famous in Britain. But as far as clock faces are concerned, the one at the top is undoubtedly the most well-known in the world. This giant of Westminster, presiding over the Houses of Parliament, is a symbol of democracy and has an hourly ring so famous that New Year's Eve and the evening news would not be the same without it. This is the clock many people around the world set their watch to. The name 'Big Ben' does, of course, refer to a large bell inside the clock tower. But it has become synonymous with the whole building. Thousands of tourists from far and wide pose for their Big Ben picture every day. The queue at a nearby red phone box for a picture containing these two British icons can take half an hour.

Standing on Westminster Bridge and gazing up at the much-loved clock face as it chimes on the hour may well be an awesome thing to do, but it's incomparable to saying you were one of the few people who have climbed the 394 steps to stand on the other side of the large, rotating hands. The first port of call for planning this rare treat is www.parliament.uk. Keep an eye out for key dates, because tickets are released in batches and sell out quickly; chances are you'll need to book at least four months in advance and be on the ball when tours become available. Getting the tickets can be tough, but it's a walk in the park compared to the slog of climbing the spiral staircase once you get there. It's not for the faint-hearted and you do need to be aged over 11, though this world class experience is undoubtedly worth the effort.

The guide takes you into the belfry, where the huge Great Bell – or Big Ben – hangs. Coming face to face with Big Ben is a strange experience. On one hand, it looks like any other big bell in a clock tower, but on the other hand it's one of the most famous bells in the world with a 'dong' that's recognisable across the globe. Be prepared for how loud it is. You're going to be up the tower when the bells chime – every 15 minutes – and it's a noise you won't be prepared for. Ear protectors are provided and I suggest you wear them. It's not just the bells that are ear-splitting; the mechanical workings of the clock are also extremely loud and provide the soundtrack to your visit. It's so noisy at the top of this tower, the bells were turned off to protect the ears of workers restoring the building over several years. Thanks to a public outcry, the ringing was switched back on for New Year's Eve. That restoration period, when 500 skilled craftsmen came here from all over the country, is another topic covered on your tour.

The clock face at the top of the tower is not the biggest in the UK, though. That record-breaking time-teller is located just down the road on The Strand atop a familiar building overlooking the Thames. The tall, white, Art Deco-style building Eighty Strand used to be known as Shell Mex House because it was home to the oil giant Shell. This huge clock face measures 7.62m (25ft), just a couple of centimetres bigger than the one on Liverpool's Liver Building, but enough to take the crown. The petrol-related business that went on in the building meant the clock was given quite a cool nickname – Big Benzene!

028

SEE LONDON'S SKYLINE FROM EUROPE'S HIGHEST FREE VIEWING PLATFORM

Number of storeys 58

Height of viewing platform 254m (833ft)

Looking through 2 storeys of floor-to-ceiling windows

View 300° of London skyline

HORIZON 22
LONDON

With so many world-famous and iconic landmarks to identify, eagle-eyed visitors to London love to get a vantage point where they can pick out key features of the capital's skyline. Between 1710 and 1963, St Paul's Cathedral was the tallest building in the capital. While climbing to the viewing deck on Sir Christopher Wren's famous dome is still an amazing thing to do and provides you with a stunning view of the city, the rise of London's skyscrapers has been a game changer for those who like to gain a perspective on the place from high up.

The Shard is the tallest building and has an awesome view from the south of the river, while the so-called Walkie-Talkie (officially the Fenchurch Building) invites people to enjoy its Sky Garden and look down on the busy streets. But when Horizon 22 came along in September 2023, its viewing platform became the highest in the city – 11m (36ft) higher than that at The Shard. That means the building at 22 Bishopsgate is in the record books and pulls

in visitors wanting to experience the highest free viewing platform in Europe. It's fabulous that this has no cost, but this does mean you'll need to book your place well in advance at www.horizon22.co.uk because this is a very popular record-breaker.

The lift to the 58th floor climbs so quickly it will make your ears pop. You leave the ground floor and within seconds you're walking out onto the

viewing platform after the super-fast elevator ride brings you to a modern, city centre perch that takes a leaf out of Manhattan's book. When the lift doors open up and you step out, staff guide you to the stunning two storey floor-to-ceiling windows that stretch around the viewing area and create an incredible panorama. On a clear day you'll see the South Downs, spot Wembley Stadium, look down upon the river meandering through the city and be able to point out the dozens of famous buildings in central London. And you'll be safe in the knowledge that there's nobody in the city getting a better skyline view than you.

The whole experience is extremely well done, making it a trip you'll certainly remember. There are interactive displays around the 300° viewing area that help you to identify spots around London and explain a little about their

history. It's a journey not to be rushed, so thankfully there's a café that can serve you up a coffee and cake while you sit and absorb the awesome vista. As for the best time to book your visit, try to get to the top an hour before sunset. That way, you'll get to see all the city has to offer in the daylight and be able to stick around as the sun dips and the first of the urban lights come on, giving this unique view a very different perspective.

029

Area 2,787m² (30,000 ft²)

Number of different storylines 65

Number of participants up to 200

Number of actors 50+

PLAY AN IMMERSIVE GAME IN THE COUNTRY'S BIGGEST OPEN-WORLD ADVENTURE

PHANTOM PEAK
LONDON

As somebody who was captivated by the movie *Westworld* when I was a kid, I was intrigued by the concept of this 'immersive world' experience in the heart of London. Bars, open spaces and a make-believe town bustling with different characters played by live actors helping adventurous folk to complete one of 65 different mystery storylines. It's a highly ambitious new approach to entertainment that you can do with friends and family – and keep going back to have a go at one of the other roleplaying games. And all without the threat of the cyborgs malfunctioning and the site going into meltdown, as happened in the film.

It's hard to describe exactly what Phantom Peak is; the premise is so unique and refreshing. At its heart, this place is a themed storytelling experience. But that doesn't really do it justice, because you – yes, you – are in the story and you wander around the setting – a brilliantly imagined steampunk-meets-wild-west town. Suffice to say that you will never have done anything like this before. And if you get enjoyment out of games, puzzles, mysteries and wacky characters, you're in for a whale of a time.

When you arrive at this fictional and yet real town called Phantom Peak, you'll soon find a bustling settlement full of people on the go. Some want to chat, others mind their own business. All spend their days alongside the many mechanical contraptions giving this place a very steampunk feel. It's like stepping inside a fantasy world, a world you're going to become very involved in if you want to solve a thrilling mystery.

First things first. You're going to need a map. You will be given one at the start of your experience, along with details on how to download an app to help you interact with townsfolk, get clues, receive advice and generally navigate your way through Phantom Peak's twists and turns. You then choose one of the dozens of interactive story trails and immerse yourself in a journey that will see you engaging both with the local characters and the environment. There's a lot going off in Phantom Peak; you could come across corporate espionage, a range of crimes and even paranormal activity. The attention to detail here is magnificent. The stories themselves are well crafted, get people heavily invested and run ever so smoothly – especially when you take a minute to appreciate how all the visitors here are at different stages in different tales.

But it's not just about the well-organised narrative. This town is very much alive with adventure and things to discover. There are lavishly designed sets, talented actors in costumes, themed steampunk toilets and even the bar gives you a chance to chat to characters and see if you can drive your journey any further. The townsfolk you come across stay in character the whole time, providing a remarkable extra dimension to your time here. This is way beyond an escape room, and way beyond theatre. The fourth wall is not just broken here, it's well and truly been demolished with a wrecking ball.

If you do need a bit of time away to gather your thoughts there's food available, games to play and even a boat ride to enjoy. And don't forget to head to the market to grab some merch.

030

FIGURE OUT WHODUNNIT AT THE LONGEST-RUNNING PLAY IN THE WORLD

THE MOUSETRAP LONDON

Opened
1952

Number of performances
29,000+

Number of actors involved
460+

Longest understudy role
15 years

The Mousetrap started life as a radio play commissioned by the BBC at the request of Queen Mary. Agatha Christie's masterclass whodunit has since become legendary around the world. The stage play has been translated into 27 languages and performed in more than 50 countries. The London version has become the longest-running play on the planet and ticket sales show no sign of slowing down. When it was first produced in 1952, Agatha Christie reckoned it would run for around eight months and then that would be that. But more than 70 years have now passed and *The Mousetrap* is still up in lights outside St Martin's Theatre. The play became the longest-running in British history as early as 1958, and every curtain call since then has seen *The Mousetrap* extend its time in the record books.

When this play opened, Winston Churchill was Prime Minister, food was rationed and TV programming ended well before midnight. They were different times. But the play, set 'in modern times', has endured and – amazingly – people turning up to see it largely have little idea how it ends. Ticket holders enter into a sort of noble agreement to preserve the longevity of the play and are asked to keep the outcome, twists and all, to themselves. For this same secretive reason, there's never been a film made of *The Mousetrap* either. An agreement is in place that one can only be shot when the London stage show has been closed for six

months. That's not going to happen any time soon. Having chalked up more than 29,000 performances and pausing only for the Covid lockdown, *The Mousetrap* is still a very well attended production.

It's a staggering number of shows when you think about it. So many plays open on the West End with a limited run; it's unusual for a play to last longer than six months. The show's success is made even more remarkable when you realise there are no 'big stars' in the cast. The audience comes for the reputation of the play. Although *The Mousetrap* opened with Richard Attenborough and Sheila Sim in main roles, it did not begin a trend of superstars in the cast. Since the first 1950s line-up, *The Mousetrap* has seen well over 400 actors tread the boards down the decades, each one adding their own depth to the play. Every

cast change leads to different interactions on the stage and a slightly different feel to the evening. For this reason, a fair few of the ten million people who have seen the show in London are returning customers.

Take a look in the foyer when you go to see this world record-breaking play. The exact number of the performance you are going to see is displayed on a wooden counter, with staff updating the number before every show. It's a popular place to pose for a photo and keep a record of which number you attended. The cast and crew take great pride in making sure this show keeps on running; when the show moved theatres in the 1970s, it did so seamlessly without missing a date. And when the scenery needed an update in 2000, this was done over a weekend to make sure no shows were cancelled.

031

CLIMB TO THE TOP OF THE WORLD'S LARGEST DOME

Roof height 50m
(164ft)

**Diameter of
dome** 365m
(1,197ft)

**Internal
diameter**
320m (1,049ft)

**Area of dome
material**
80,000m²
(861,112ft²)

THE O2 ARENA
GREENWICH

You may recognise the O2 Arena from its regular TV appearances on opening credits to *Eastenders*. Or maybe you can remember it featuring in the James Bond adventure *The World is Not Enough* when 007 Pierce Brosnan ended up on the roof. Perhaps you've been to a concert inside the venue, or were one of the six million visitors who went along to the millennium exhibition it was built to house in the year 2000. I visited what was then called the Millennium Dome in that first year, and while the year-long event received a lot of criticism in the media, you couldn't help but be impressed by the architectural imagination and sheer scale of the structure. Although not a true dome in the precise nature of the word because it is held up by the 12 iconic yellow pillars, the Guiness Book of Records does recognise this East London landmark as having the biggest dome shape of any building on the planet.

Rebranded as the O2 Arena, the dome now houses what is commonly recognised as the busiest music venue on Earth. It's hosted over 2,000 events, which have brought joy to millions of people. The biggest acts in the world come here to perform to audiences of 20,000, and several bookings have become record breakers in themselves. Prince arrived in

2007 and played an unprecedented run of 21 consecutive nights, something that took a huge amount of stamina and has not been topped. Two years later, Michael Jackson was due to play no fewer than 50 sold-out shows, but this residency never happened due to his untimely death. The shows here benefit from cutting edge sound and light technology, but it's not

just music delighting the masses here; the arena has hosted NBA and NHL games, along with several exhibitions.

You can have a stunning, record-breaking experience on top of the dome as well underneath, though. Not all the action at the O2 takes place on the inside. For a truly adventurous visit to the O2 Arena, get kitted out with safety equipment and walk from one side of the dome to the other, climbing to the top of this huge structure and carefully making your way back down to terra firma. It's known as 'Up at The O2', and it's a lot of fun. Not only will you feel the rush of adrenaline as you conquer the world's biggest dome but you'll also have time to pause and take in a unique view of the capital city. From here you can see Canary Wharf, the whole of Greenwich, the Olympic Park, and beyond. What's more,

you can choose what time to book your urban adventure, seeing the London skyline early in the morning, during the day or in the evening. Each time of day has its own special nuances, with the light bringing out different features of London's famous skyline.

You'll be shown the ropes (literally) before you begin your trek up the dome's walkway, and your instructor will be up there with you at all times to make sure you're both safe and having the time of your life. There are plenty of viewpoints in London, but few have a USP like this one. The feeling you get on the top of the O2 Arena is second to none. This is a big dome and it produces a big feeling. Have a look at www.theo2.co.uk/up-at-the-o2 for all the different booking options, including a romantic private deal for those who would like to propose to a partner on the top of the dome.

032

Number of skulls
1,200

Size of the pile of bones 7.5m (24.6ft) long and 1.8m (5.9ft) tall

---

Number of bodies here
2,000

Origin
7th century

ENJOY A MACABRE VISIT TO THE UK'S LARGEST COLLECTION OF HUMAN SKULLS AND BONES

ST LEONARD'S CHURCH, HYTHE, KENT

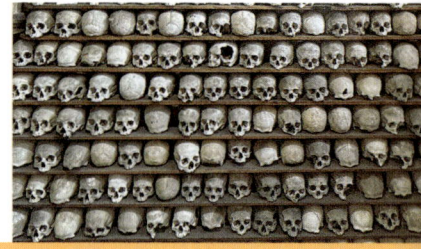

In the quaint and picturesque town of Hythe, close to Folkestone on the southern Kent coast, a lovely church holds a grim collection within its walls. Down in the crypt, on shelves, hundreds and hundreds of human skulls are piled up on top of each other, gazing out at any tourist who ventures this deep. The skulls offer nought but a hollow stare; the visitors reciprocate with jaws ajar and eyes wide open. For this is no ordinary sight.

Being confronted by over a thousand ancient human skulls in the eerie setting of a crypt is enough to make the hairs stand up on the neck of even the toughest customer. Shelf after shelf is packed tightly with skulls, all sharing the same human features and yet all with their own individual differences that add character and perhaps a story to their stoney exterior. It's the skulls, the faces of people long gone, that grab all the attention here, but the crypt is also full of other human bones. Stacked up against a wall in a neat display, they reach from floor to head

height and stretch on for over 7.5m (24.5ft). This is the largest collection of human skulls and bones in the country, and rivals some of the larger and more famous skull collections in the world, such as Hallstatt's in Austria.

This fascinating space in St Leonard's Church was referred to as a 'charnel house' in the 17th century. Such places were found where burial grounds were in short supply; bodies were interred for five years until decomposition had taken place, then the bones were stored inside

the building so other bodies could be laid to rest. It's macabre stuff, I'll grant you, yet there are few places in the world that have such an eerie display. This makes it oddly compelling. It's a haunting, unforgettable experience.

It's not known exactly when this collection was first installed, but there are written references to it in 1678 and 1679. The earliest known drawings were made in 1787, and they show the bones piled high inside the door. Sketches from the early 19th century reveal the crypt in those days was in pretty much the same shape as it is in today.

So just who were the people who make up this record-breaking collection inside a pretty Kent church? A number of theories over the years have piqued the interest of history fans. Were they Danish pirates killed in a battle? Perhaps

men who fell in the nearby 1066 Battle of Hastings. Or maybe Anglo Saxons killed in battle? Possibly victims of the Black Death? These are all mightily impressive theories, some of which have written evidence to support them. But there's nothing like a good scientific study to dampen the flames of the most inspiring speculation. Between 2009 and 2012, research into soil traces found within the skulls concluded they were buried locally – as early as the 13th century. These were likely ordinary folk who lived and died in the Hythe area over a long period of time, though speculation remains over whether some of them travelled from Europe due to the size and shape of the skulls. We may never know. And I guess the lack of clarity adds to the intrigue surrounding this most unusual record-breaker.

033

STROLL TO THE END OF THE WORLD'S LONGEST PLEASURE PIER

Length 2,158m (7,080ft)

Opened 1830

Material hardwood decking, iron pillars

Alternative transport train

SOUTHEND PIER

The best way to process just how far Southend Pier stretches out to sea is to set off on the lengthy stroll to the end without turning around. As you wander by the attractions and tread these historic wooden boards, don't be tempted to glance back to the coastline. Not until you stand by the railings at the far side, over 2km after you set off. And then, when you finally do catch a glimpse of the Essex city in the distance, it'll take your breath away. The pier reaches an almost impossibly long way out to sea, rendering Southend a small, distant vision on the horizon.

This record-breaking attraction is not just the longest pier in the country, but the longest pleasure pier in the whole world. It's so long that many don't really fancy walking all the way to the end because of the amount of time it takes, and some will get to the end and run out of steam for the journey back. Thankfully, there's a small train that regularly runs the length of the pier and will take you some – or all – of the way. The Pier Railway will have

you at the end in around ten minutes. The most popular pier-related activities can be found either at the shore end or at the head of the pier. The section between the two is a thin conduit with more of a design focus on practicality rather than entertainment. I guess it would be a very challenging task to make it all as action-packed as a Blackpool pier for its entire length. Southend's pier is just too long for that.

British piers are symbols of the Victorian era when seaside tourism was on the rise. They provided places to walk, rest, take refreshments and play amusing games. Southend Pier, though, was built as much more than an attraction. This structure jutting into the water was a means of arrival, designed to lure day trippers from the capital by boat. The 19th century civic leaders wanting to increase tourist spending in Southend identified a problem when they discovered boats were leaving London and bypassing Southend in favour of Margate. The vast sands at Southend mean it's very hard for ships to land here. But not if there is a pier 2,158m – or 1.34 miles – out to sea, where the water is deep enough to allow boats to moor and visitors to disembark. From here, they could be whisked down to the shops in no time.

Southend's pier is a fascinating and iconic feature of the city's skyline and has stood proud for nearly two centuries. It's welcomed thousands of visitors and been a major boost for Southend's economy, but it's not all been plain sailing. The wooden boards have made it susceptible to fire and there have been several blazes that needed significant repairs. In 1959, a fire hit the pavilion near the shore and trapped 500 people on the pier. All needed rescuing by boat. In 1986, a tanker collision ripped a gap between the pier head and the rest of the structure. It was three years before visitors could walk to the end again. But every time it has suffered damage, Southend Pier has bounced back and it remains the iconic, record-breaking symbol of Southend.

034

THE SCENIC RAILWAY DREAM-LAND, MARGATE

Opened
1923

Length 914m
(2,998ft)

Height
12m (39ft)

Top speed
60mph

It's not the fastest and it's not the longest. It doesn't aim to make you scream and it's not going to turn you upside down. But what Margate does have in the historic and much-loved Dreamland amusement park is the oldest roller coaster on these shores. Opened in 1923, having taken three years to build, the Scenic Railway offers an insight into what cutting edge technology was like over a century ago when British coastal resorts were all the rage and visitors started demanding more from their day trips. It remains a key feature, still effortlessly putting smiles onto the faces of the riders, but in a very different way to the white-knuckle rides designed today. Back then, the trend was for roller coasters to provide descents down gentle slopes, nice views from lofty positions and well-designed, themed displays.

Stepping on board the Scenic Railway is like stepping back in time, experiencing all the fun of the fair like the people used to in the roaring 20s. Two climbs during the ride hoist you up to an elevated position and then you're off, quickly tackling gentle slopes as your tummy experiences a nostalgic tickle. Dreamland operates on a token system; you buy some and exchange them for a go on the rides. Each attraction costs one token, except for this classic ride; you'll need two to get a seat on the Scenic Railway.

One of the key features of the Scenic Railway is that it's made out of timber. The whole ride is a wooden construction, as they

all used to be. This adds a super sense of historic charm to the experience. Just seeing the timber frame is pretty magical. Riding over it, hearing the clackety-clack of the carriage, well, that's something else. A roller coaster made of wood, however, does not come without risks. Fire has been an issue several times at the Scenic Railway. In 2008, the ride was severely damaged by a blaze and had to close.

But the Scenic Railway is more than just a ride in Margate. It's an iconic symbol of the town's history as a seaside tourism giant and a record-breaking big name in the theme park world. It was no surprise, then, that a meticulous restoration project was begun to bring the famous roller coaster back to life keeping to the original design, as demanded by its status as a Grade II Listed Structure.

And in 2015 it reopened, as good as new and welcoming first-time and returning riders to experience the century-old journey.

Dreamland itself is full of historical wonder. It was created as a tourist attraction to pull folk into Margate from London as the railways were chugging into action during the 1870s. Early entertainment in what was known as the 'hall by the sea' was laid on by circus impresario George Sanger, and a host of fun things to do were introduced. Dreamland today caters for the modern audience and is a major music venue, attracting many top performers. Whether you're turning up for a party or an ice cream, do take a ride on the Scenic Railway. It's the beating heart of what is one of Britain's oldest seaside amusement parks. Find more to do there on your day trip at www.dreamland.co.uk.

035

EXPLORE THE WORLD'S OLDEST (AND BRITAIN'S LARGEST) STONE CIRCLE

AVEBURY STONE CIRCLES AND HENGE

Diameter 331m (1,085ft)

Age 4,600 years old

Number of stones originally over 100

Inside the stone circle a cracking pub!

Mention stone circles to somebody doing a tour of Britain and they're bound to mention Stonehenge, or maybe Callanish. They're the classic British stone circles, the ones that appear on the cover of guide books and woo foreign tourists out of London to the countryside. Fabulous and unmissable though these stone circles are, neither holds the record for being either the oldest or the largest. They don't even come close. For there's a stone circle in the UK that dates back 4,600 years and is so big, you can't photograph it all in the same shot. Set your Strava as you begin a walk around the edge of Avebury Henge and you'll see it's a good, long stroll to get all the way around. And it can take you a few hours to properly explore everything there is here.

Avebury's large outer stone circle has a diameter of roughly 331m (1,085ft), dwarfing other sites such as Stonehenge. Smaller stone circles can actually be found within it. This complex layout highlights the ambition and scale of planning needed by those setting it down. The stones are, quite simply, massive. The biggest of the circle's stones weighs 100 tonnes (220,462lbs) and is the heaviest in

Britain. Excavations have shown it to extend down more than 2m (6.5ft) into the ground. The tallest of the stones can be seen at the north-east of the henge and, like the others, is a locally sourced sandstone known as sarsen. Just how they were brought here, and exactly what the henge was used for, remains a mystery. Maybe it always will, and perhaps that's part of the appeal.

Further wonderment was added to this site in 2003 following an archaeological survey that found there were no less than 15 huge monoliths buried below the ground in the middle of the circle. You are free to wander around the site and explore the many different stones that stand in this awe-inspiring space, but be respectful and consider their historical significance. The size of the henge means there is a large area of land in the middle of the stone circle and, unlike other sacred sites, this one is actually utilised by today's humans. Part of the village of Avebury was actually built inside its extraordinary ring of stones. There's even a beautiful village pub in the middle of it. The Red Lion has an old well within its walls; arrive early to bag the seat above it.

The complexity of Avebury's stone circle again sets it apart from its peers. It's thought there were once 100 stones here, though some have been lost or taken away over the centuries. There's also a large ditch and embankment that formed part of the henge; the ditch was once an incredible 9m (30ft) deep and the embankment was made from the chalk material that was dug out. Both the ditch and the embankment would have been white at the time they were created, and both added layers of complexity to the site.

But that's not all. The significance of this stone circle extends well beyond the village itself. The henge sits in a wider Wiltshire landscape, which is home to several ceremonial and ritual sites. For a start, there's West Kennet Avenue, a row of paired standing stones connecting Avebury's henge with a site known as The Sanctuary. The rolling countryside around Avebury is indeed full of mystery and intrigue.

036

BECOME THE WORLD'S BEST CONKER PLAYER

First title 1965

Number of competitors 400

Number of conkers used 2,000

Fundraising total £420,000

Amount of skill needed absolutely none

WORLD CONKER CHAMPIONSHIPS SOUTHWICK

What was something of an art form back in the day has become an almost forgotten ritual in many parts of the country. The simple schoolyard battle of conker vs conker would once upon a time attract a cheering crowd gathered around two kids trying to smash the other's horse chestnut with brute force and add victorious numbers to their own conker's tally. If your conker had ten points and beat a conker with 30 points, you suddenly became the owner of a 'conker 40'. Competition was intense. Some of my mates were rumoured to have soaked theirs in vinegar and baked them in the oven in an underhanded way to make them harder. Such blatant cheating would surely have resulted in a lifetime ban if this was an Olympic sport. You can still see young children collecting conkers as the spoils of an autumnal walk, but you'll do well to see any threading string through one and playing the game. It hardly ever happens in the Game Console Age.

But things are different in Southwick, where the game of conkers not only lives on but positively thrives. Every autumn as the leaves are turning and the air gets a chill, as many as 5,000 people gather for the World Conker Championships – a nutty contest that crowns the King and Queen of Conkers and raises money for charity at the same time. Pay your entrance fee at this autumnal festival and it could literally be you who becomes the world champ. All you have to do is defeat a few rivals and smash your way to victory. How hard can it be? Very hard, is the

answer. This is a game of chance more than skill. There are local folk who have been taking part for years without a sniff of becoming Conker royalty.

Randomly placed against other competitors in round one, you choose a string poking out of a black bag to select your conker – you can't bring your own or even see the one you're going to use. There's no room for cheating in a contest this important. You then stand on a podium and start your game, with other bouts going on around you. There's a toss of the coin to see who goes first and then each person gets three chances to hit the other conker. Taking turns at every three attempts, this lasts for five minutes before going to a conkers version of a sudden death penalty shoot-out. If your conker is the first one to smash then you're out of the competition, with the solace of knowing you can now head for the bar. But if you're victorious, you get a ticket to take part in the next round.

I blasted my way into round two with relative ease and was having some solid strikes against my second opponent when disaster struck; even though it was my shot and I hit their conker with power, it was my conker that disintegrated and sent me crashing out of the knockout championships. And that was it. I had to wait until the following year to have another go. I hope your attempt to grab this world-beating achievement will be more successful.

Check dates and register for the championships online at www.worldconkerchampionships.com.

037

DISCOVER ANCIENT ARTEFACTS IN THE UK'S OLDEST MUSEUM

Opened 1683

Number of coins
300,000

Number of ancient Egyptian pieces
50,000

Total number of objects
1.2 million

ASHMOLEAN MUSEUM OXFORD

Oxford is a renowned seat of learning and home to one of the oldest, most reputable and consistently high-achieving universities in the world. It's perhaps fitting that the oldest museum in the country, and the world's oldest university museum, should be located in the heart of the city. The name is taken from the man we have to thank for inspiring the museum in the 17th century. Elias Ashmole donated his extensive collection of manuscripts, books, curiosities and coins to the university in 1677. Six years later, the museum opened its doors so members of the public could see them. Over the decades, the collection was expanded significantly and is now housed on Beaumont Street, in a building it moved to in the 19th century

Among the most popular galleries are those dedicated to ancient empires. This is one of the leading places in the world to encounter relics from the ancient Egyptians, and anybody with an interest in this fascinating period of history can spend an enjoyable afternoon here. The range of artefacts at the Ashmolean have given archaeologists an insight into what rituals and beliefs were typical in ancient Egypt. The

oil paintings from the tomb of Nebamun are brilliantly preserved and show what daily life was like at the time.

No matter how much fun kids have learning about Egyptians at school, no matter how many documentaries you watch on history channels, nothing can really prepare you for coming face to face with an actual Egyptian mummy. The

mummified remains of Meresamun are jaw-dropping, beautifully preserved and here for anyone to see free of charge. We know a little about Meresamun because of an inscription on the front of her coffin. She was a singer in the interior of the Temple of Amun, an elite musician priestess. Music played an important role in pacifying the gods and Meresamun made music for Amun. We know she came from a wealthy background because of the way the coffin is richly decorated with a wide range of colours and symbols. Along with the Egyptian artefacts, Meresamun allows us a rare glimpse into the past and a chance to get genuinely excited about history.

The ancient Greeks and the Romans also have a considerable presence in the Ashmolean. Beautiful Greek vases compete with stunning Roman mosaics and sculptures to be the standout piece of artwork here. We'll call it a tie. Combined, they show the incredible artistic talent and achievements found in these ancient civilisations. The statues of the Parthenon are among the most attention-grabbing pieces, but do spare time for the smaller objects in display cases. These items of jewellery and everyday objects sometimes tell us most about the daily lives of the ancient Greeks and Romans.

Two other things to look out for on your trip to the country's oldest museum are coins and musical instruments. There are over a quarter of a million coins kept here in an incredible collection from a huge range of time periods and cultures, telling fascinating stories about economies and politics. The musical instruments on display date as far back as the medieval period.

038

Number of life-size dinosaurs
220

Dan-Yr-Ogof discovered 1912

Number of skeletons found in Bone Cave
42

Creatures once living here
hyenas, wolves, cave bears

THE NATIONAL SHOWCAVES CENTRE FOR WALES

In a remote valley beneath the Black Mountains of South Wales, not too far from Merthyr Tydfil and Swansea, there have been strange sightings among the trees. Talk of dinosaurs, rumours of a T-rex, claims of seeing a Diplodocus. Could this be true? Welcome to the National Showcaves Centre for Wales, a brilliantly presented attraction in a fantastic setting. The centre has more than its fair share of jaw-dropping, stunning caves beneath the surface, along with an attention-grabbing, record-breaking collection that steals the show on the surface. And with a children's play area also on site, families should plan to be here for a full day before heading home with heaps of fond memories

The range of life-size dinosaurs on display in the grounds is fabulously impressive. This is the largest collection of prehistoric models in Northern Europe and at the same time is one of the best in the world. Animatronics bring the creatures to life as they move their heads and bodies, while sound effects do their best to transport you back in time 65 million years or more. This is also a learning experience, though.

Information on the different animals comes at you thick and fast, meaning there's loads to soak in for budding palaeontologists. Did you know, for example, that the T-Rex could scoff a whopping 230kg (507lbs) of meat in a single bite? Look out for your favourite dinosaur, or it may be that you leave the dino display with a new favourite you hadn't realised until now. You'll need to keep an eye out above your heads

for the terrifying pterosaurs as well as focussing on the bushes and trees for the diverse collection of carnivores and herbivores.

Visitors should, of course, try to visit the attractions both above and below the surface of the Earth here in South Wales. There are three main cave areas to discover, each with its own features and natural beauty. First up is Dan-yr-Ogof, which contains some rare and unusual formations, now known as the 'angel' and 'rasher of bacon' due to their appearance. It was in 1912 when the Morgan brothers went caving down here by candlelight that they discovered Dan-yr-Ogof after a long and difficult crawl through the rock. As you might imagine from such a grand name, the Cathedral Cave is quite a sight to behold, huge and decorated with thousands of fragile 'straw' stalactites. Discovered by members of the South Wales

Caving Club in 1953, it's home to many unusual landforms and subterranean waterfalls cascading into underground lakes. Dreamy.

In the appropriately-named Bone Cave, no fewer than 42 human skeletons were discovered. These remains are thought to have been here for over 3,000 years, which would date them back to the Bronze Age. They were all found in the main chamber of the cave and among them were silver rings, pieces of bronze jewellery and evidence that Romans also used the area. As you walk to the entrances of all three caves and gaze on the grounds from their lofty entrances, look out for more dinosaurs. They are seemingly everywhere in what is a stunning, ambitious collection of intriguing reptiles.

039

Number of annual visitors
250,000

Rocket tower height 42m (137ft)

Planetarium capacity
192

Cost of construction
£52 million

HAVE AN OUT OF THIS WORLD AFTERNOON AT THE UK'S BIGGEST PLANETARIUM

NATIONAL SPACE CENTRE LEICESTER

It seems our fascination with outer space knows no limits. Be it going to see the latest sci-fi blockbuster at the cinema or diving into a good book, exploring what's going on beyond our planet is as popular as ever. In the week I am writing this, one of the biggest solar flares in recent memory has triggered a stunningly beautiful northern lights display that saw the skies turn green and purple as far south as Sheffield. That evening, as word got around on social media, hundreds of people were lining country roads close to where I live in the hope of getting a rare glimpse. All too often, however, adventures of this kind are curtailed by light pollution and clouds. So what you need to fulfil your curiosity is a visit to the largest planetarium dome in the country – and lots of other space-related displays – at the National Space Centre in Leicester.

There's much to get excited about on a trip to the country's premier space centre. But undoubtedly, the highlight has to be your allotted time in the Sir Patrick Moore Planetarium. Named after the legendary BBC TV presenter who did so much to promote the solar system (and beyond) through

The Sky at Night, this huge area ramps up the anticipation as soon as you enter. Comfy seats angle you to gaze at the ceiling where a huge screen curves throughout the dome, ready to educate and entertain.

There are various shows you can watch, one of the most popular being *We Are Stars*, narrated by Gollum actor Andy Serkis. He is the voice behind the Time Master character, a Victorian gent with a time travelling tent taking you back 13.8 billion years to explore our origins. *We are Aliens* asks if there is other life out there and if we will ever meet it; this one being voiced by Harry Potter's Rupert Grint. And David Tennant gets involved in the narrating for a show called *We Are Astronomers*. All these shows are well worth checking out and will captivate you from start to finish.

Look out also for the live stargazing shows, where expert astronomers will point out and guide you through the constellations and everything else of interest. These events are great because there's an interactive element where you can ask questions about things that baffle you about the cosmos.

Whichever way you approach the National Space Centre, the first thing that will catch your eye is the huge rocket tower. It's mightily impressive and houses another record-breaker – the tallest vertically stored rocket in the UK. The Blue Streak and Thor Able rockets that are housed in this purpose-built tower are truly awe-inspiring. Climbing to the different levels of the rocket is incredibly rewarding. If you ever fancied a journey into the stars, the best the Space Centre can offer is a virtual ride on a craft leaving from Tetrastar Spaceport. Take your seats for a beautiful ride among the stars, and one that will be a learning experience. There's a lot going on at the Space Centre and you can check out the special events at www.spacecentre.co.uk.

040

GET IN A SPIN WITH THE MOST INVERSIONS ON ANY ROLLER COASTER

Number of loops
14

Height 30m
(98ft)

Top speed
52.8mph

G-Force
+4.5G

THE SMILER ALTON TOWERS

With more thrill-seekers passing through the turnstiles than any other theme park in the UK, Alton Towers has earned its reputation as being top of the pops for white knuckle rides. The park has always been pushing the boundaries of what people expect from their roller coasters, and innovation has long been the name of the game here. But it may surprise you to learn that Alton Towers has been pulling in paying guests since the 1860s. The Earl of Shrewsbury laid on a range of attractions on the site and opened up his extensive gardens to raise funds.

It wasn't until 1980 that it became famous as a theme park, inspired by Disneyland and boasting the magnificent Corkscrew as one of its first rides. That early, iconic thriller featured one inversion and became synonymous with the park as it grew in popularity. But the decades have slipped by and now one inversion just isn't enough. Part of the original Corkscrew track welcomes visitors at the entrance like a dinosaur fossil in a Natural History Museum. Today, everybody wants to ride The Smiler, a mesmerising experience that will put you in a topsy turvy trance thanks to its 14 (yes, 14) summersaults. It boasts more inversions than any other ride in the world.

When I rode The Smiler, the hype surrounding it had helped build up a bit of anxiety about what was to come, made slightly worse by the wait and listening to the thrill-induced screams of those on the ride. As it shot off, the inversions started quickly and never seemed to relent.

I wasn't always aware of when I was going upside down or not; the whole ride became a disorientating blur. I do remember thinking, as the ride stopped at the halfway point, that I'd had enough. That I wanted to get off. And then it all began again in reverse, with seven more inversions. When this lengthy ride finally came to standstill, my friends said I looked green. And while I managed to keep my lunch down, I did learn that The Smiler is one tough ride. The G-Forces and the inversions you experience really are like nothing else. But I did it and will happily keep the bragging rights.

New rides that Alton Towers open are often shrouded in secrecy until their big launch. And these multi-million-pound projects usually contain a USP that makes other theme parks green with envy. When the spooky ride TH13TEEN first glided around the Forbidden

Forest zone of the park, it was the world's first freefall drop roller coaster. And what a cracking experience it is, full of thrills and surprises. Before that, one of Alton Towers' signature roller coaster, Oblivion, became the first ever vertical drop of its kind anywhere in the world. Oblivion is still something to behold, both when you watch it plummet down the track from the viewing area and when you are strapped into one of its seats. The secret to the thrill is the way the ride pauses before the drop and you're told, 'Don't look down'. After being held suspended for what seems like an eternity, the ride then descends into a tunnel specially built to allow the ride to meet planning requirements; the authorities don't let Alton Towers build higher than the surrounding tree line and the only way to accommodate Oblivion was to go subterranean.

041

MAKE A SPLASH ON THE FIRST TRAPDOOR WATER SLIDE

THUNDERBOLT, WATERWORLD STOKE-ON-TRENT

Begins with a trap door opening to a vertical drop

Flume speed 25mph

Number of slides 20

Number of pools 3

If you're looking for one of the most adrenaline-pumping experiences in the UK, head to this water park in Stoke, if you dare! Waterworld is an all-action indoor water park that goes further than most by including high-speed thrills as you've never experienced before. Opened in 1989, this attraction has been a big deal in Stoke for some time. But a big investment in 2019 saw four new rides open in a section of the park named Tornado Alley, transforming the whole place into a much more white-knuckle venue that now pulls in 400,000 visitors a year. Waterworld is nothing to do with the Kevin Costner film of the same name, incidentally, so no need to worry about a pirate posse marauding around like it's at the end of civilisation. You're more likely to come up against excited families jostling in the queue for another go on Thunderbolt.

Created for the waterpark's 30th anniversary, Thunderbolt is the premier attraction in Tornado Alley. It's the highest waterslide you're going to find anywhere in the country – measuring in at nearly 17m (55ft). Oh, and did I mention it begins with a scary vertical drop? As your watery journey begins, you step into a sealed booth, standing on a blue trapdoor you know is going to give way in a matter of seconds and plunge you into a massive adrenaline rush. Standing there, arms crossed over your chest, waiting for the operator to press the button, may only take a couple of seconds but it can seem like an hour. And then you drop, straight

into a fast-flowing flume of water that carries you along at 25mph through a twisting tunnel that plays havoc with your senses. The first thing many people do at the end is head up to join the queue again.

Tick off Thunderbolt and you'll want to have a go at the others. Cyclone will see you sit on a rubber ring and be propelled into a torrent of water, completing the twisting route through two giant bowls at no less than 19mph. Make sure you also save time for Stormchaser. Another fabulously named adventure to keep up the extreme weather theme, this is the longest ride in Waterworld and one that takes you through a series of tunnels at great speed, some of them in darkness and others with a festival of lights to keep you mesmerised. The three rides in Tornado Alley might be the attention grabbers but together they make

up just a fraction of the overall attractions at Waterworld. There's so much going on inside this record-breaking waterpark that you're going to have a fun-filled day.

And to extend the adventure further you can visit the on-site mini golf or the new immersive, Staffordshire-themed Adventure Mini Village for those with younger children.

042

Number of seals
10,000

Number of pups born each year
4,000

Length of spit
6.4km (4 miles)

Summer visitors
thousands of terns

Not summer visitors dogs

BLAKENEY POINT
NORFOLK

The north Norfolk coast is a constantly changing landscape where the North Sea batters and erodes the shoreline with every high tide. At some places, the soft cliffs are being eaten away at an alarming rate, threatening local communities. The process of longshore drift, however, has led to the creation of a lengthy spit at Blakeney Point. Deposits laid down by waves over hundreds of years have made a long finger of sand and shingle that points out into the sea. The sands of the spit can be shifted by storms, but during calmer weather it's a popular place for walkers. And it's also home to the country's biggest colony of grey seals.

Blakeney Point is an ideal seal refuge. It's a sheltered area and there are no natural predators for the seals to be concerned about. The sandy spit has no shortage of space for them to use, and there's plenty of food available in the North Sea. No wonder, then, that thousands of seals arrive here every winter to give birth. There are so many grey seals visiting these shores between October and January, the National Trust has given up trying to count them all on the ground. There are simply too many to keep a track of. Late autumn and winter are the best time to see the seals, though there will be some who hang out here throughout the year. The summer, though, sees the area become a hotbed of activity for thousands of terns and oyster catchers, many of them nesting on the ground. With this stretch of our coastline being such a wildlife asset, dog-walking at Blakeney Point is restricted for most of the year.

Although a wander along the spit is a real joy and not to be missed, another rewarding way to encounter our largest seal colony is by boat. Make your way to nearby Morston Quay and hop aboard one of the boat trips that set off along the river towards the spit where the seals are. You benefit from getting a ride straight to the heart of the colony and a view of them that's second to none. The seals love to lay about close to the water's edge and there will be plenty darting in and out of the sea as well. The boats get you into a unique seal-spotting position. Visit www.beansboattrips.co.uk for more information.

Seals enjoy a fascinating public image that belies some of their extremely dangerous characteristics. We're used to seeing cute and cuddly images of gorgeous seals on calendars and posters. Maybe you've also come across a fluffy soft toy, a beautiful white seal you can embrace and give a hug. The reality is very different. Some time ago, walking on the beach, we came across a young seal we thought looked in distress, isolated, whining and quite a way from the sea. A local walker called a seal expert and they were soon on the scene, properly equipped with extremely thick gloves among other things. Seals, we were told, have a ferocious bite, packing more pressure per square centimetre than some large dog breeds. The upshot is this: don't get too close to the seals, both for their protection and yours. Keep to the designated areas and take a pair of binoculars for your close-up look. If you spot an injured seal, call the British Divers Marine Life Rescue on 01825 765546.

043

CHUG ALONG BRITAIN'S LONGEST SURVIVING HERITAGE STEAM RAILWAY

Length 49 km
(25 miles)

Commercially open 1922–37

Fully preserved line opened 2011

Stations 16

WELSH HIGHLAND RAILWAY PORTHMADOG

A picturesque steam train chugging through the North Wales countryside, harking back to the country's industrial past. It might be considered the archetypal Welsh view. And yet many think the railway line linking Porthmadog and Caernarfon was one of the biggest white elephants in Welsh history. Opened in 1922, the line was riddled with problems from the outset, not least the 19th Century carriages customers had to endure on the long journey through the mountains. The services ran for just 15 years before closure saw the line fall silent. Restoration plans surfaced in the 1960s, but it was not until 1991 when reopening as a heritage line saw passengers riding the rails once more. Section after section was preserved and reopened, with the whole line available for tourist exploration from 2011.

For those who have never experienced the thrill of watching a steam engine leave a station or, even better, sitting on board and seeing the clouds of steam engulf the windows as you pick up speed, this is an activity that must be put on your 'to do' list. Spending an afternoon on this satisfyingly long heritage railway is something that everyone can find fun in, from the excited six-year-old to the nostalgic 88-year-old. The

Welsh Highland Railway often delivers even more than visitors are expecting, especially when you book in for a seasonal special to ride with Santa or the Easter Bunny. Sitting in the carriage, being pulled up the Welsh slopes, you'll experience a real bombardment of the senses. The sound of the whistle blowing. The smell of the coal burning. The classic noise of the engine pulling away and the carriages trundling along

behind. The world class scenery drifting by the window. Taking a trip on this – the longest heritage railway in the UK – is an unforgettable treat. For anybody of a certain age, the sight of a steam train among the Welsh mountains will bring back memories of Ivor the Engine. It was a simpler time, when a very basic cartoon of a train and a dragon captivated young audiences in all corners of the country. Well, spending an afternoon on a steam train in north Wales is like stepping back to that simpler time, letting Ivor the Engine do the hard work. And was that a Welsh dragon you just saw up there among the summits?

It's amazing to think people objected to these futuristic steam engines chugging through the countryside when they were rapidly being developed in the mid-19th Century and early 20th Century. People don't like change, I guess.

Today it would be unthinkable, though, not to have these iconic Welsh steam locomotives moving slowly against the horizon. And we have an army of supporters to thank for bringing this line back to life in a journey that took several decades. Today, the Welsh Mountain Railway is dependent on volunteers and welcomes anybody who wants to become more involved, either by giving up their time or chipping in and becoming a member. Currently, there are more than 1,000 people signed up to dedicate a small annual fee that helps keep the wheels a rolling. The number of volunteers available will often determine if the timetable is operating with steam engines or a diesel engine. To make sure you get the steam experience, check ahead. www.whr.co.uk.

044

FLY DOWN THE WORLD'S FASTEST ZIP LINE

Top speed
100mph

Length 1.5km
(0.93 miles)

Height
500m (1,640ft)
above the quarry
lake

Zip wire width
16mm (0.62
inches)

VELOCITY
BETHESDA

An abandoned slate quarry on the northern outskirts of Eryri National Park now echoes with the joyful screams and exclamations of thrill-seekers taking part in a range of fun activities. The ultimate one on this site at Bethesda is Velocity, a long zip wire adventure that sees you careering from the top of a Welsh mountain, soaring over a lake and reaching record-breaking top speeds in the process. Yes, the adventurous team at Zip World have transformed this beautiful industrial monument into a place where family and friends can get their hearts racing and maybe face a few demons.

After getting kitted up with a harness, helmet and goggles, it's a short walk to a practice run. This starter is a relatively tame zip line across the quarry's lake, which is mainly to get you used to the process of taking off. The first step is laying down on a bed, where staff will fasten you to the line and get you into the flying position – legs stretched out horizontally, hands by your side holding one of the straps. The bed disappears, there is a countdown in Welsh and you wonder what on earth you've

let yourself in for. And then you're off, at quite a leisurely pace.

With the dress rehearsal completed, you climb on a truck and begin your ascent of the mountain. It becomes apparent as you climb the old quarry track at seemingly impossible angles for about 15 minutes that this run is going to be different. And then, before you know it, you're taking your turn in the launch area, looking at the crazy distance to the end point, the

ludicrous angle of the zip wire and the people before you vanishing to a small dot as they reach 60mph in less than 10 seconds.

When it's your turn, make the most of this incredible experience. Take it all in, as you fly over the cliff-edge, gaze down at the blue-green waters below you, feel the air blast your face as you gain speed, and look at the tiny people and sheep below you. The scariest bit is when you approach the end and you're slowed down by the brakes on the line. But even this is extremely well managed and not something to worry about. And if you want to relive the experience, you can buy the video of your thrilled face that's been captured by a camera on your helmet since before take-off.

It's fair to say not everyone in our group was looking forward to flying down this record-breaking zip wire. My wife was having second thoughts and did contemplate not going through with it. But there was a huge smile on her face when she landed at the end of the run, and I reckon she'd do it all again. All the staff working on the site – and there are plenty – were wonderfully reassuring. When you're about to be fired off a mountain top with your life dependent on a thin wire and the proper safety precautions being taken, listening to them talk about 'cross checks' is exactly what you want to hear. Even if there is the odd joke dished out about how to swim out of the lake if it goes wrong. So cast aside any fears you may have and become one of the world's fastest zip liners! Book your flight at www.zipworld.co.uk.

045

Elevation
1,085m

First climbed
1639

Routes
6 main hiking
paths and 1
railway

**Summit
temperature**
10°C cooler than
the Welsh coast

SCALE THE HIGHEST MOUNTAIN IN WALES

YR WYDDFA ERYRI NATIONAL PARK

Towering above its mountainous peers, the peak of Yr Wyddfa is a Welsh icon that over 600,000 people climb every year. This record-breaker provides a real sense of achievement for those who make it to the top, and, with a railway to the summit, it's one of the most accessible mountains you'll find. It's a destination that has grown in popularity over recent years and some would say it's simply too popular; on occasions, the crowds have put extreme pressure on footpaths and facilities. The mountain is more often known as Snowdon and the national park as Snowdonia, but the Welsh names Yr Wydffa and Eryri have been officially adopted and will, in time, become the norm.

As with any challenging mountain, it's not enough to simply turn up without any planning. You need to know your route, you must be dressed for the weather and arrive early enough to secure a place in one of the very busy car parks or catch the right bus. All the routes to the summit are challenging and require a good level of fitness. The most popular path leaves the slate grey town of Llanberis on a 9 mile (14.4km) route that is

probably the best one for those who have not tackled the mountain before.

A far more difficult way to the top is on the Miners' and Pyg tracks that are a lot steeper in their ascent and cover some rocky terrain. One of the longest, steepest and most difficult climbs up Eryri can be taken up the Watkin Path. Parking is very limited at the start of the path and this one is not recommended if it's

your first time or you have limited mountain experience. But it's definitely one to tick off for the more experienced climber.

There is, of course, a much easier way to get to the summit. If you're unable (or unwilling) to tackle the difficult hike to the top, take a seat on the Snowdon Mountain Railway, and enjoy the ascent in comfort. The station at the summit is, unsurprisingly, the highest in Britain. Try to pick a clear day when the summit is not shrouded in cloud so you can enjoy the views, which get better and better as you ride the steep 4.7 mile (7.5km) journey from Llanberis. The rails are an amazing example of ambitious Victorian engineering, transporting tourists here since 1896, and ensuring that the famous Welsh mountain is accessible for everyone. However you get up, you may well be pleased to discover that there's a well-stocked visitor centre and café awaiting you at the top. Few mountains have this kind of facility, though few have a railway to keep it supplied. After getting your refreshments, head to the triangulation pillar that marks the summit. Depending on how busy it is, you may have to wait your turn here to get the obligatory trig point photo. But on a clear day, many would say this is the best place to be in Wales.

Responsibility is the key word for people visiting Yr Wyddfa within Eryri. Treat the area with respect and take all your rubbish home with you so that adventurers in the future can have the same wonderful experience as you

046

CAREER DOWN A MOUNTAIN ON THE UK'S FIRST (AND ONLY) ALPINE COASTER

FFOREST COASTER BETWS-Y-COED

Route up
365m (1,197ft)

Route down
710m (2,329ft)

Max gradient
25 per cent

Journey time
6 minutes

Invented during the 1990s to add some summer fun to mountain resorts, the alpine coaster has become one of the hottest adrenaline experiences to bag. Towns and villages in the Alps were used to an influx of tourists during the skiing season, but when the snow melted most of that infrastructure lay unused. Hikers made use of some cable cars to get a lift up to the mountain ridges, but if you built a coaster and added a downhill bike track, then the natural gradient of the landscape could be a big draw for adventurers all year round. Some of the coaster courses in the world's big mountain ranges are something to behold. Andorra boasts a 3.3 mile (5.3km) track in the Pyrenees, Switzerland has a course where coaster fans start the run at 3,300m (10,826ft) above sea level, and participants reach up to 26mph on a track called 'The Pipe' in British Columbia, Canada.

Given that the UK has several mountain ranges, it's a wonder it took until 2017 for an alpine coaster to open on our shores. Sure, there are toboggan runs, but the alpine coaster is quite a special creature – a fixed metal ride onto which cars are fastened and controlled only by brakes. The Fforest Coaster in North Wales is the first – and only – alpine coaster in the UK and it is a joy. There's over 1km (3,280ft) of shiny track and you're pulled up the first 365m (1,197ft) through the leafy forest, gaining height and getting yourself ready for the exhilarating glide down. Sit tight and think yourself lucky you don't have to walk up to the starting point.

There are no ski lifts here that could be used, like in the Alps, so the circular route is planned to perfection as it effortlessly takes you high up the mountain. And then the thrills begin, with gravity sweeping you down the hill on a twisting and turning course that sits very close to the ground so as to give you an enhanced feeling of speed.

Passing beneath the track you have just come up on, the course weaves back and forth to make the most of the gradient on the downhill section that runs for 710m (2,329ft). You do get thrown from side to side fairly awkwardly on the turns, controlling the sledge with the brake. The first time you attempt the downhill hill coaster run you tend to be fairly cautious as you get to know how to control it and where the route takes you. But when you buy your ticket for this adventurous afternoon, you are

paying for three goes. By the time you get to the last run you're feeling a lot more confident in your abilities and can have a decent attempt at your personal best time. You can get up to speeds of around 25mph, though obviously you're in control of how quickly you want to whizz through the forest.

This one is for almost all the family. Thrill-seekers as young as three can get on board with an adult taking control of the brake. As soon as your kids are aged nine or over, they can have their own sledge. In the wilds of North Wales, of course, the weather can take a turn for the worse but the many trees around the course tend to do a good job sheltering you from the wind. If it's raining, there are canopies to fit over the sledge to keep you dry. Plan your trip at www.zipworld. co.uk/adventure/fforest-coaster.

047

BRAVE THE WORLD'S FIRST TANDEM DROP EXPERIENCE

PLUMMET BETWS-Y-COED

The drop
30.4m (100ft)

Number of people plummeting one or two

Experience length
20 minutes

Nerves needed
titanium level

I've experienced thrilling drops before, so I thought I was prepared for plummeting. There are drop rides at most theme parks. I'd done a high ropes activity and taken the 'leap of faith'. And if you, too, had experienced these kinds of drops and thought nothing could challenge you further, it's really time to write a new bucket list. Because Plummet is next level.

You'll find it at beautiful Betws-y-Coed, where forests grow tall, waterfalls crash, and tourists enjoy some of the best facilities North Wales has to offer. This is a perfect place to base yourself for a weekend in the national park, so it's an ideal place for Zip World to have some of their adventurous attractions. And Plummet is a top notch one in this outstanding part of the world. This is not a tree-based activity, even though you're high among them as you take part. No, a special tower has been built for this one, giving you sufficient height and – crucially – an unforgettable experience leading up to

your plummet. You reach your all-important platform by climbing a set of steps that lead up the tower. At the top, you're attached to your safety harness and, when it's your time, led to the platform. On the floor there are two sets of footprints indicating where you need to stand. You can do this solo or bring a friend along to share your anxiety at this point.

Apart from the distance you fall, the platform is the real difference between this drop experience and the others you may have tried. Firstly, this is not a 'leap of faith' thing; you

don't have to jump and you're not in control of when you drop. At some point the trapdoor you're standing on will open. There is often a countdown to let you know the big moment is on the way, but you can choose to do it with absolutely no warning if you have nerves of steel. And when the trapdoors open, that's when you and your partner plummet over 30m (100ft) down to the ground. Now obviously, with a trapdoor and a fearful drop, there are parallels between this experience and the gallows, and you do feel a little like Captain Jack Sparrow as you stand there waiting for your destiny. It all adds to the anticipation and adrenaline rush.

The whole experience takes around 20 minutes, from your safety briefing to the final free fall. It's cheaper to tackle Plummet as a pair, though you can book a single ticket. Groups are welcomed, and these often have very interesting dynamics as folk start to lose their nerve when they see what other people have experienced. There are, of course, some nice views at the top of the tower. But, to be fair, enjoying these will most likely be the last thing on your mind as you grit your teeth and get ready for a thrilling plummet to earth.

048

TEE OFF AT BRITAIN'S ONLY UNDERGROUND GOLF COURSE

UNDERGROUND GOLF LLECHWEDD SLATE MINE

Number of holes
18

Temperature 7°C

Duration
90 minutes

Number of floors
4

Back when I was a kid, it was called Crazy Golf. These days it's known as Adventure Golf and it's easy to get on board with the rebranding when you see some of the courses on offer. The technically difficult, immaculately kept, indoor courses today require large investments and are simply a joy to play. There's nothing crazy about them. This is altogether more serious stuff, while at the same time being a lot more fun. Urban centres are now home to a fleet of pirate and tropical island themed obstacle golf courses, along with the odd risqué adult-only party golf venue. But if you head into the former mining communities of North Wales you'll find a truly original adventure golf course, the likes of which you'll not come across anywhere else.

Deep inside the former Llechwedd Slate Mine, close to Blaenau Ffestiniog, there is a challenging 18-hole golf course suspended in mind-bogglingly deep caverns. Against a background of steep, subterranean slate cliffs, lit by purple and green lights, the adventure golf course is split over four levels and you follow the route up and down steps to complete the challenge. Anybody who

has enjoyed a game of mini golf before will know the score: you get a couple of clubs and attempt to sink the ball in the hole using as few strokes as possible. Getting in your way are slopes, barriers, dips, holes and buildings, many with a slate mine, industrial theme to make you feel at home in this incredible underground space. You must negotiate links of chains, saws, machinery and iron girders en

route to getting a low score, preferably one below par.

Of course, things don't always go to plan and there'll be times when you make a hash of things. Again and again, if you're anything like me. Don't worry, though, because netting at the side means that you're unlikely to send your ball careering down into the abyss, no matter how bad you are! But rules are rules, and if you have six shots you have reached your max and move on to the next hole. On the other hand, get a hole-in-one and you're morally obligated to buy everyone a round of colas when you reach the surface!

Getting the tee for hole number one involves taking part in another record-breaking activity. To get down in the old slate caverns you need to descend on an old, industrial

cable railway that is officially the steepest in Europe. It's on this that workers used to head down to their shift and come back up to the shower block. The Llechwedd course is, indeed, the first underground golf course to be established inside a cave and the huge space, combined with the futuristic and imaginative lighting, helps to create an eerily impressive activity. If you think the first few holes are straightforward, that's to lull you into a false sense of security. As you descend the levels and head deeper into the cave, the challenges get tougher.

You'll also be able to learn a thing or two about the mine's history, with information being cleverly intertwined with the 18 holes. At the end, you can choose to either work as a team or compete with your mates to try and set the 'explosives' off in another fun challenge.

049

Depth 419m
(1,375ft)

Rooms 4 cabins
and 1 grotto

Temperature
10°C

Wifi amazingly,
there is

DEEP SLEEP BLAENAU FFESTINIOG

Beneath the mountains of North Wales, hidden away in the labyrinth of an abandoned Victorian slate mine, a handful of people are enjoying an extremely deep sleep. They are occupying beds that have an entire mountain rising above them, snugly experiencing the unparalleled darkness and constant temperatures you can only find underground. To be precise, the adventurous overnighters are some 419m (1,375 feet) below the surface of this national park. For here, where men once grafted to extract slate needed for the world's roof tiles, you'll now find comfy mattresses, fairy lights and even a decent wifi connection. Welcome to the Deep Sleep Experience, possibly the coolest place on the planet to rest your head and get 40 winks. With a mountain of rock above your head, you can say goodnight to insomnia caused by noisy neighbours, stormy weather or heavy traffic.

Many accommodation providers attempt to brand their services with a unique selling point, but few can truthfully declare something as magnificently individual as this. The Deep Sleep experience is not part of a hotel, and nor does it claim to be. Instead, this is an 'adventure camp' where you go on an underground expedition and spend the evening with a small group of other thrill-seekers.

It's more about living life on the edge rather than in the lap of luxury. The evening begins at 5pm when you're taken on a 45-minute hike into the mountains and then, after getting kitted out with a helmet, boots and torch, you enter the old slate mine and start an hour-long, steep scramble over rocks, bridges and staircases until you are over 400m (1,312ft) beneath the surface.

Then you can put your feet up somewhat. There'll be a hot drink and tasty meal made for you, all enjoyed with other guests at a large picnic table. Your accommodation will be in a simple cabin with twin beds, unless you're feeling really flush and go for the posher grotto option with a double. You can enjoy a peaceful evening, but don't expect a late check-out; you'll be up and away at 8am, climbing your way through the mine's passages and getting back to the car park by 10.30am.

This is one of the most unusual places to sleep anywhere on Earth and you'll doze off knowing that you're the only people camping this far down. The lighting at the camp is powered by batteries charged by flowing water in the mine. The toilet is similar to a composting loo. There's no doubt that you're staying off grid a long way down in a mountain. And so, when the lights go off, you will experience total darkness. What you won't get (unless you're in the grotto) is total silence. The Welsh mountains are notorious for receiving buckets of rain throughout the year and that water filters down through the ground and into the mine slowly and steadily. Expect to hear trickles, drops and, sometimes, gushing waterfalls. It all adds up to an extreme experience like no other and a deep sleep you'll remember forever.

050

SAIL ACROSS THE HIGHEST CANAL AQUEDUCT IN THE WORLD

PONTCYSYLLTE AQUEDUCT

Materials
iron and stone

Length 307m
(1,007ft)

Height
38m (125ft)

Opened
1805

**Number of piers
standing in water**
4

Before the railway revolution thundered into cities, towns and villages across the country, engineers charged with improving the transport of goods and materials were turning to our waterways. One ambitious plan to boost the boating network in Wales and western England included linking the River Mersey with the River Severn to connect Liverpool with Shrewsbury and gain faster access to important coal fields. The Ellesmere Canal was therefore devised. One of the toughest challenges for the boffs in charge was how to span the River Dee just outside Wrexham. The canal had to be kept dead level across the vast vale the boats needed to navigate. The result was the stunning Pontcysyllte Aqueduct that to this day – over 200 years later – remains a world record-breaker.

Stretching on for 307m (1,007ft), the 7-metre (23ft) wide aqueduct is carried across the Dee on the back of 18 arches. As it turns out, the dream of creating the full Ellesmere Canal was never completed. The expense of the aqueduct threw the larger project into doubt and this was the last major work to be completed. Before long, the rumbling railways consigned canals to history.

Today it's known as the Llangollen Canal and this section offers an important glimpse into our industrial heritage. You can take a narrowboat trip across the aqueduct – or walk across it if you can stomach looking at the big drop down to the river.

Head into the visitor centre for all the information you need about the aqueduct's origin,

construction and rejuvenation. There's even a model of the aqueduct for you to have a go at building, and this is much harder than it looks. Make sure you get the right number of piers in the water and the towpath is consistently on the correct side. There's no charge to go into the centre or walk across the aqueduct itself, though donations are welcome. Call ahead to check availability for the boat trips that take you across and head a little further up the canal before returning.

Tucked away in the Welsh countryside close to the border with England, the aqueduct is away from large areas of population and it's easy to think it would be overlooked by visitors in favour of other attractions. But this is not the case at all. The immense structure that carries the canal over the River Dee in the Vale of Llangollen is of global significance. It's listed as

a World Heritage Site, putting it on the same footing as historical buildings in Rome and Athens. When I arrived at the site and started to walk across the lengthy aqueduct, one of the first people I got speaking to was a woman from Perth, Australia, who was on a tour of Northern Europe and had made this the very first destination on an international trip. The folk marketing Welsh tourism are doing a great job to make sure the word is getting out, and that's not surprising given that this is both the highest canal aqueduct in the world and the longest in Great Britain.

Along with some smaller aqueducts that help the canal to negotiate the undulating relief of North Wales, the canal provides some fascinating walking country. UNESCO described this World Heritage Site as a 'masterpiece of creative genius'.

051

THE RACECOURSE GROUND WREXHAM

First international game 1877

Number of international games to date 90

Highest attendance 34,445

Home team Wrexham AFC

Experiencing a new rush of fame thanks to the Disney+ TV show *Welcome to Wrexham*, the Racecourse Ground has long been in the record books as the oldest international football ground still in use. It first held a match between two countries in 1877 when Scotland travelled to Wrexham for the first ever home game involving a Welsh national team. Since then, a Welsh captain has led the team out onto the pitch at the Racecourse Ground 90 times. That's more than any other stadium to have hosted a Wales international. Some football grounds to host many Welsh games – such as Ninian Park – have been demolished, but the future looks bright for the Racecourse Ground. Investment in new facilities is set to increase the capacity in the wake of Ryan Reynolds' and Rob McElhenney's purchase of Wrexham AFC.

Among the international football games held at the Racecourse Ground since 1887 are clashes against Ireland, England and Gibraltar. Rugby Union matches have also been staged here, with Wales taking on the likes of the USA, Australia and Italy. During the Rugby Union World Cup in 1999, the Pool 4 game between Samoa and Japan was played here, and the ground has also hosted several large pop concerts. Since Motörhead took the stage here in 1982, Stereophonics, Olly Murs, and UB40 have all headlined summer gigs.

Getting a ticket for a Wrexham match at the Racecourse Ground is not as easy as you may think. The Hollywood glitz and Disney+ factor

have put bums on seats here and even made sure away teams sell more tickets than normal. Add a series of successful seasons to the pot and you've a Welsh recipe for sell-out crowds. To snap up any spare tickets you'll need to be registered as a member, or maybe you're lucky enough to have your local team playing an away match against Wrexham. Despite its long history, this is not an antiquated ground; it's modern and equipped with good facilities, from the footy scran available to the items in the well-stocked club shop.

Arrive in good time to go for a drink in The Turf pub, which sits right next to the stadium and is entwined with the rich footballing history of the stadium. It was here that Wrexham AFC was established in 1864, and, although there have been many changes at the stadium, the pub has remained a constant that has welcomed

generations of fans down the decades. The TV series *Welcome to Wrexham* followed the ups and downs of the club in the years after the much-publicised Hollywood buyout, with The Turf being one of the key venues for filming.

Expect a queue to get in before kick-off on a match day; this pub is extremely popular among fans, as well as more neutral spectators now it's been on TV. It's a decent size once you're in, and as well as serving beer, the pub acts as a museum for the club. Every nook and cranny of this fascinating pub reveals a new insight into the history of the football club. And despite holding the record for international games, the main business of this historic football stadium is, of course, looking after Wrexham AFC who play all their home matches here. Get tickets at www.wrexhamafc.co.uk.

052

Height 310cm
(122 inches)

Width 182cm (71 inches)

Depth 305cm
(120 inches)

Cost in 1891
£20

CROUCH INSIDE THE SMALLEST HOUSE
IN GREAT BRITAIN

THE SMALLEST HOUSE CONWY

You've heard of people downsizing, but this is going quite to the extreme! In the gorgeously picturesque town of Conwy on the North Wales coast, a petite house stands with a grand reputation. This is officially the smallest dwelling in Britain; a teeny tiny residence that just about manages to squeeze a bedroom upstairs and a living area on the ground floor. It's located on Lower Gate Street and ordinarily it would be easy to miss because of its diminutive size, but somehow its bright red paint makes it stand out like a beacon. Buy an entrance ticket (at www.thesmallesthouse.co.uk) and you can cram inside to see what it was like to call this miniature end terrace 'home'. Living here looks almost impossible, and to be fair nobody has lived here permanently since 1900. But people did squash into this tiny dwelling in the 19th century, before one insightful owner stopped it from being demolished by suggesting it could have a great future as a tourist attraction.

Let's talk about the dimensions first of all. They are ridiculously tiny. If you've baulked at the space given to some new builds or student accommodation, this will reset your thoughts. Standing on the road, looking at this tiny terrace that seems bolted on to its neighbour, it's a little

over 3m (9.8ft) high and well under 2m wide. Step inside and you'll find the house is just 3m (9.8ft) deep, meaning even the most inventive interior designer would have a tough job on to maximise the living area. According to the census information, several people lived here

over the decades, including fisherman George Edwards, master mariner William Jones, and a painter by the name of Phillip Davies.

A local landowner and fisherman called Robert Jones bought the house for £20 in 1891 and it came with a sitting tenant – also called Robert Jones. A copy of the conveyance can be seen on the wall inside the house when you visit. Robert Jones (the tenant) continued to live in the house until 1900 when the local authority said it was unfit for inhabitation and ordered its demolition. Not pleased by this, Robert Jones (the owner) argued it could provide an income as a tourist attraction and set about proving that it was the smallest house in Britain. He travelled all over the country measuring other small houses that had the same claim and eventually achieved his aim; this tiny terrace entered the Guinness Book of Records in the early 1920s and to this day it remains in the ownership of Robert Jones' family.

This record-breaking house was built to fill up a wasted space and to help alleviate the shortage of housing in the town at the time. Two rows of houses were built along the town walls near the quay, each started at the towers at the opposite end of the street. But they didn't meet in the middle, so one entrepreneur builder took advantage of the situation when he realised the space only needed a roof and a front wall to become a dwelling.

053

BREAK OUT OF PRISON AT THE WORLD'S LARGEST ESCAPE ROOM

Built 1877

Number of cells 173

Maximum number of inmates 326

Number of hangings 7

SHREWSBURY PRISON

Thankfully, most of us will never experience what it's like to spend time behind bars, which is the precise reason why it's quite appealing to venture inside an old gaol and play a game about breaking out. While being sentenced to time for real is not something to aim for, there's something absurdly fun about playing at it, safe in the knowledge you'll be let back outside when your session has finished. And so get ready to be sent down, in a Kafka-esque way for a crime you did not commit, at Shrewsbury Prison's Escape Room.

The first thing you have to do in this amazing, record-breaking experience is confess your crimes as you're booked into the prison. From this moment on, you leave your name behind and are given a number instead. And then it's time to put on your standard issue orange jumpsuit so you look the part before being taken to the main hall for some of the ground rules. From here, the prison wardens – who look just like the real thing – will take you to your cell and lock you in. This is when the game begins.

It's the ultimate escape room experience, trapped inside a highly secure prison. You're locked away and pretty much forgotten about. And you're not going anywhere until you have a watertight solution. Or until your time runs out, when you will be allowed to leave but you'll have to do the walk of shame out of your cell. More than half the people have to do this because the games on offer are so challenging. Well, you wouldn't expect anything less from the world's biggest escape room, would you?

There's more than one escape room experience available at Shrewsbury Prison, with the ultimate being the Prison Break event that gives your team an adrenaline-pumping two and a half hours to get your act together. Of course, the fact you're in a real prison is at the forefront of your mind all the time and it definitely adds a thrilling dimension to your event. I've been to escape rooms in old office blocks and other, more mundane venues, but this setting just cannot be beaten. It's a historic building with a fascinating history. OK, it wasn't designed with the intention of giving you and your mates an entertaining afternoon and I'm not sure what 19th century inmates would make of it, but I can see a pleasing irony in today's visitors having fun within these walls and being allowed to go home without clearance from a judge.

Built in 1877, there were male and female convicts sentenced to porridge here until 1922, when it became male only. It operated until 2013, at which time it was a category B prison. Over the decades, several men were sent here for carrying out gruesome crimes; and no fewer than seven were hanged here for murdering women. As part of your experience, you will learn a lot about the prison's history and some of the events that unfolded here. But there are also other unique things to do here, which you could combine with your time at the record-breaking escape room. You could enjoy a bit of jailhouse rock, for example, on the nights when the prison is transformed into a bar. Or if you really have nerves of steel you could sign up for a night behind bars when you sleep in one of the cells that once housed the criminals of the past. Book your spot behind bars at www.shrewsburyprison.com.

054

TAKE A TOUR AROUND BRITAIN'S LARGEST CATHEDRAL

Height 101m
(331ft)

Length 189m
(620ft)

Area 9,687m²
(104,270ft²)

Number of bells
14

LIVERPOOL CATHEDRAL

Towering over the city of Liverpool, the stark, monumental cathedral may not win awards for being the prettiest place of worship but it's certainly one of the most imposing. Built from red sandstone quarried in the south of the city, this gargantuan cathedral took much of the 20th century to complete. The key stone was laid in 1904, with initial plans being more gothic in design and containing two towers at the cathedral's west end. A replanning in 1910 opted for a less ornate exterior and the one central tower we are now familiar with. A service to mark the completion of Liverpool's now-famous cathedral was held in October 1978, with Queen Elizabeth II in attendance.

Standing beside this stunning Grade I Listed Building and gazing up, it's hard to understate the sheer size of Liverpool Cathedral. This is, put simply, one of the biggest and grandest religious buildings in the world. So, let's get to grips with the dimensions and record-breaking aspects of Liverpool's Church of England cathedral. For a start, it's easily the largest cathedral in Britain. It's actually the biggest religious building of any kind on these shores. It's also the longest cathedral in

the world, measuring 189m end to end. When it comes to overall volume, this is the fifth largest cathedral on the planet. Towering 101m (331ft) up from the ground, it is also one of the tallest non-spired cathedrals anywhere and holds its own among the increasingly futuristic city skyline, being the fourth tallest of all buildings in Liverpool. It's not, however, the only cathedral in Liverpool; just half a mile along Hope Street you'll find the smaller Roman Catholic Cathedral.

As soon as you step inside this gritty, towering building, you leave the noise and bustle of the city behind and find yourself in a sanctuary, with calming rows of fine columns stretching out before you and natural light pouring in through stained glass windows. Make your way to the Lady Chapel. It's a real highlight, a smaller space with intricate carvings that is there for you to engage in peaceful prayer and reflection should you wish to. The main area for worship in the centre of the cathedral is known as the Great Space, and for good reason. It's a powerful and immersive place to spend time and is the regular focus for worship, reflection and celebration. This is a modern, 20th century cathedral that manages to match much older religious buildings for size and grandeur, while having a more grounded design at its heart. It seems the perfect fit for the city of Liverpool.

If you've got a head for heights, make sure to build in a trip to the top of the cathedral's iconic tower. This has to be one of the best things to experience in your visit to the cathedral, where you can make the most of its commanding position to reach the city's finest vantage point. Ascending in two consecutive lifts and then climbing up a 108-step spiral staircase, you're brought out at a viewing platform with astonishing views across the city. Gazing out over the River Mersey, from this unique place, you can also take in much of the surrounding countryside and pick out key landmarks such as the Liver Building. It's a spiritual experience that brings you closer to this vibrant and fascinating city. Learn more at www.liverpoolcathedral.org.uk.

055

WALK AROUND THE MOST COMPLETE CITY WALLS IN THE COUNTRY

CHESTER CITY WALLS

Age of the oldest sections 2,000 years

Number of main gates 4

Number of towers 7

Height up to 12m (39ft)

Thickness up to 3.7m (12ft)

There's only one city in Britain where you can walk around almost a full circuit of city walls. Chester still retains its ancient defensive structure, some parts of which are, incredibly, almost 2,000 years old. And you're still able to take a stroll along the top of them, just as folk in Chester have done for centuries, even millennia. Circumnavigating the city walls in Chester is a rewarding and memorable experience. Not only does it connect you directly with the city's history, but this is also a brilliant way to get unrivalled views of Chester.

The most popular way of getting up onto the top of the walls from street level is at the four main gates that once provided access into the city – Northgate, Eastgate, Westgate, and, frustratingly for the perfectionists out there, Bridgegate. Steps between the main gates also provide a route up to the top. A walk around the entire length of the walls will clock up two miles (3.2km), so it's a decent stroll over some uneven surfaces that can take the best part of an hour, or longer if you stop to admire

Chester's landmarks and pop back down into the city for refreshments.

It was the Romans who first made attempts to build the defensive walls, protecting the fortress Deva Victrix with earth and wooden structures. The next major fortification came following the Norman Conquest when a castle was built on a site outside of the original Roman defences. The city walls were extended to the west and south so the new fort could be protected, and this is

where the city walls remain today. Despite being trampled on and used for recreation – as they have been for centuries now – this is still very much a historic monument that needs regular upkeep, so do treat the walls with respect.

There are several things to look out for on a journey around the city walls, all of which offer a glimpse into Chester's awesome history. Start with the Eastgate Clock, said by some to be the second most photographed clock after the faces surrounding Big Ben in Westminster. It's a very ornate affair and you may not be surprised to learn it was put up to commemorate Queen Victoria's Diamond Jubilee in 1899. You'll see it standing above Eastgate. Heading north from here you'll see the Roman Gardens on your right, a well-kept display with Roman columns and an underground heating system. It's a reminder of how closely linked Chester was to the Roman Empire.

Up next is Phoenix Tower, also known as 'King Charles' Tower', with a little museum inside detailing the role it played in the Civil War. Turning left, you'll soon reach Northgate and get a cracking view of Chester Cathedral and the gardens. Further along, look out for Bonewaldesthorne's Tower and the Water Tower, the latter being linked to Watergate, though not the one connected to Richard Nixon. You can reach the Rows from here, the city's famous and architecturally fascinating two-tier shopping street. And don't miss the Wishing Steps a little further along the walls. Run up and down these without taking a breath and your wish will come true, according to local legend.

056

HAVE SCOOPS OF FUN AT THE WORLD'S LARGEST ICE CREAM SHOP

THE ICE CREAM FARM CHESHIRE

Number of flavours 50

World first ice cream drive-in

Make time for mini golf

Open daily

It's one of life's simple pleasures, isn't it? A crispy cone packed with several scoops of mouthwatering ice cream. Lick the top and savour the taste, but don't take too long over it or you'll have melting issues to deal with. There's a traditional British idea that an ice cream is best enjoyed on the coast during a summer's day, but things have changed in the world of frozen dairy treats. A growing number of farms have diversified into creating delicious ice cream. It's a brilliant development that means you can enjoy a top quality cone all year round.

By far the biggest of these tasty developments is The Ice Cream Farm, a place with a self-explanatory name that has been officially crowned the biggest shop of its kind in the world. The parlour itself could keep you busy for the best part of an afternoon, depending on your appetite and budget. But there's plenty more going on at this Cheshire attraction, which puts on family events and has many options for youngsters who like adventurous play, including mini golf, a race course, and an area for sorting

gemstones. The kids can have a fabulous time while you finish off another scoop... or three.

The parlour is a lovely place to enjoy your ice cream, but make no mistake – a trip here is all about the flavours. It's likely to be your biggest, most difficult, and most important, decision of the day. If you're indecisive when it comes to making sweet choices, it might be best to have a look on the website beforehand so you aren't too bewildered on the day when faced with a

whopping array of frozen delights. Perhaps it is best to go for a two or three scoop option. Variety is the ice of life, as they almost say. Personally, I'm tempted every time to go for the Biscoffi, although toffee fudge and salted caramel are also up there battling for the cool top choice.

For those looking for something totally different, try ordering marshmallow flavour, which actually contains delicious chunks of marshmallow. There's also unicorn flavour, though presumably that doesn't contain delicious chunks of unicorn. Another speciality is the mixed flavours. How about rhubarb and custard? Liquorice and blackcurrant? Apple and sour cherry? Whatever your taste in ice cream, there is sure to be a flavour (probably lots of them) that suits you. After all, a typical day at the Ice Cream Farm has over 50 different

ones on sale. And there are plenty of options also for ice cream lovers who are vegan or have a dairy-free diet. Vegan vanilla, chocolate and coconut are just some of the choices, and that's before we get onto the sorbets. There's a high chance of you freezing at the front of the queue because there are too many nice tastes to enjoy.

But that, of course, is why you're likely to be tempted back here on another visit. If you want to enjoy some of the ice cream at home, tubs are available to buy and take with you. And if you're in a rush, there's even a drive-through option. However you end up sampling ice cream from the largest shop of its kind, you'll discover the award-winning Cheshire Farm Ice Cream is a joy. Choose your flavours at www. theicecreamfarm.co.uk.

057

DIVE HEADFIRST INTO THE UK'S TALLEST BUNGEE JUMP

TATTON PARK
CHESHIRE

Height 91m (300ft)

Available selected weekends

Jumping from a crane

Bragging rights unlimited

Once you're hoisted over 90m (300ft) into the air and have completed safety checks at the top of a huge crane, you'll have a few seconds to enjoy the view. In the heart of Cheshire, Tatton Park, near Knutsford, is a brilliant location with rolling parkland and plenty to keep you on the lookout. If only you had more time to take in this awesome landscape. Alas, before you know it, it's your time to make the leap of faith. That is, you have to launch yourself off your platform of security and plunge towards the excited folks gazing up at you with anticipation from the ground. Welcome to the UK's tallest bungee jump, which sees daredevils plummeting down towards Cheshire, only to be rifled back up into the air just before they make contact.

Bungee jumps were first seen by westerners during World War II when indigenous people on Pentecost Island, in Vanuatu, tied lianas to their ankles. The modern format of this extreme pastime was invented at Bristol University's seemingly crazy Dangerous Sports Club. Somebody had the idea of jumping off the Clifton Suspension bridge wearing a top hat and tails while carrying a glass of champagne. And why wouldn't they? While for many that may seem like an idea born of Bedlam, it turns out this was a blood-rushing activity that actually caught on. Big time. Before long, adrenaline-seeking tourists heading to New Zealand, Australia and the USA were coming back with stories about jumping off bridges into beautiful

canyons, safe in the knowledge that they had some elastic tied to them so they would at least bounce back before reaching the ground.

The people taking the leap at Tatton Park are not doing so off a bridge into some idyllic valley setting. They're jumping from the top of a massive crane towards a country park, so it may not be the stuff of dreams for those after the adventure traveller experience. But this is as daring and incredible as bungee jumping can be in the United Kingdom. It is the biggest distance that you can plunge on these shores, and doing so will take more than your fair share of bravery. And it's not just about having the courage to get off the platform and start falling through the air, it's about how you do it. I mean, you're not going to fly but ideally you want to be falling with style, as Buzz Lightyear said. The boasting rights at the end will be off the charts.

This jump, on the outskirts of Manchester, will see you make the brave leap and drop down towards the country park. You can either make the jump on your own or in tandem with a buddy. The crane making all this possible is not on site every day, so if this is a record-breaking activity you'd like to tick off you should scoot along to www.ukbungee.co.uk and find out which is the next weekend they are taking bookings for. Get yourself signed up if you fancy telling mates you've dived off the UK's tallest bungee jump platform!

058

First recorded game 1667

Match length up to 11 hours

Distance between goals 3 miles (4.8km)

WATCH THE WORLD'S OLDEST (AND EXTREMELY DANGEROUS) GAME OF FOOTBALL

ROYAL SHROVETIDE FOOTBALL ASHBOURNE

Arrive in Ashbourne, Derbyshire, on Shrove Tuesday or Ash Wednesday and you can tell something is afoot. While the rest of the country is busy making pancakes, the residents of this town on the edge of the Peak District have been busy barricading shop windows, removing cars from the streets and putting up warning signs that vehicles, bikes and property might be damaged. It's as if Ashbourne is fearfully getting ready for a riot, but actually there is excitement in the air as final preparations are made for the world's oldest competitive game of football.

And yet the precautions are not taken in anticipation of football hooliganism; the shops are protected in case they're damaged in an event the town comes out to watch and celebrate. And the whole town is out. The pubs are packed, but most other businesses are closed. It's more hotly anticipated than Christmas in Ashbourne. The clash between two opposing halves of the town has been held almost every year since at least 1667 and the place pretty much shuts down for an extended celebration.

This is not your typical football match, for there are hardly any rules. Officials state there must be no murder or manslaughter, but almost everything else is fair game. You can kick the ball, pick it up, run with it, swim with it, pretty much anything. That is in the unlikely event you get anywhere near it. Most of the time, the ball is at the centre of a massive scrum with dozens of people pushing from the back in order to gain vital ground. Anything that gets in the way of the scrum is likely to be severely damaged,

from shop windows to cars and council flower displays. This is not due to wanton vandalism, but instead sheer focus and dedication to win the game. For that time in Ashbourne, there is nothing more important.

Folks on one side of the town are known as the Up'ards and the other are the Down'ards. The ball is lofted into the air at 11am in the main square from a specially built pedestal, and then the aim is to get the ball into the opponents' goal. The two goals are three miles (4.8km) apart. I wasn't lying when I said it wasn't like any other football match. As soon as the ball is loose, the players try to grab hold of it and surge in the direction of the goal. Sometimes there's no sighting of the ball for long periods of time as it remains hidden in a scrum of more than 50 people. Then, all of a sudden, it will pop up and players try to get it to their speedy

runners who want to gain some valuable ground en route to the goal.

On the day I went along, the ball ended up in the river for a good couple of hours, a scrum of steaming men fighting for the ball in the water. It was also kicked into a lake on the edge of the town, with players immediately diving in and trying to gain an advantage by swimming with it towards the goal. Each game is totally different and the ball can go in any number of directions in such a large playing area. If a team scores a goal before 6pm, the game is restarted in the market square. A goal after 6pm stops the game, though play is potentially allowed to continue until 10pm. You can follow the action around for as long as you like, taking in a historic game of football like no other.

059

WALK THROUGH THE BIGGEST CAVE ENTRANCE IN BRITAIN

PEAK CAVERN
CASTLETON

Height 18.2m (59.7ft)

Queen Victoria visited in 1880

Main chamber 100m (328ft) long

Unusual use concert venue

Picturesque Castleton in the English Peak District is pretty much on the border between the Dark and White Peak. About a mile (1.6km) to the north, the gritstone and peat creates a very different landscape to the limestone and farming country south of here. Castleton itself has limestone as its bedrock, a permeable rock susceptible to erosion that has resulted in a labyrinth of underground streams and caverns. The result is some of the most wonderful and strange features you'll see on these shores – huge subterranean spaces adorned with stalactites and stalagmites surrounded by 350-million-year-old fossils and rare minerals.

And at Peak Cavern, close to the foot of the beautiful Winnat's Pass, you will be able to stare up in awe at the largest cave entrance in Britain. It is huge. The arching entrance is nearly 32m (104ft) wide and over 18m (59ft) tall. Buy your ticket (www.peakcavern.co.uk) to go inside, see many interesting natural features, and get an insight into the old craft of rope-making that was practised here for decades. As recently as 1915 there were actually families living here within the cave,

troglodytes who made a living manufacturing rope for local mining industries.

In a clever marketing strategy that amuses children of all ages, Peak Cavern has started to go by the name of 'The Devil's Arse'. You'll see this on the large sign enticing people in from the main road through Castleton, and on the website. If you want to peer inside the Devil's Arse you can access it by strolling up a passage that leads up the hill from the car park.

But, you might well wonder, where on Earth did such a strange name come from? Well, although the good people of Peak Cavern have only recently switched to this fun name, it may surprise you to hear that it does, in fact, date back to the 19th century. This cavern was known as the Devil's Arse by visitors and locals because of the strange, trumping noises that could be heard emanating from the cave by the people in the nearby village. This unromantic sound of breaking wind was caused by underground rivers filtering down through the cracks in the depths of the cave, much like the water in your home might gurgle as it makes its way down the drains. And so Devil's Arse was the cave's name. But then Queen Victoria decided to make an official visit to the cave, and it was correctly assumed she would not be amused. Managers were seemingly fearful of Her Majesty turning up and having to say

'Welcome to the Devil's Arse, Ma'am.' And so they changed the name to 'Peak Cavern' and it remained that way for over a century.

During the summer months, the cavern doubles up as a unique concert venue benefiting from awesome acoustics and a stunning atmosphere. Sheffield legends Richard Hawley and Jarvis Cocker have both played here. But make sure you come here from the traditional roadside entrance. Once, while I was here watching John Shuttleworth, the comedy gig needed cancelling because one ticket holder was stuck at the top of the cave entrance, clinging to a tree in need of a mountain rescue team. They were staying in a nearby village and decided to walk to the cavern across fields following a map on their phone. Not recommended.

060

CLIMB TO THE HIGHEST POINT IN
BRITAIN'S OLDEST NATIONAL PARK

KINDER SCOUT
DERBYSHIRE

Elevation
63m (2,086ft)

Prominence
497m (1,630ft)

**National Park
established**
1951

**Number of trains
per day to Edale**
18

The green, rolling dales and dark, moody moorland of the Peak District are often seen as less challenging hikes than the summits and dramatic glacial landscapes of Scotland, North Wales, or the Lake District. But the picturesque villages and quaint climbs of Derbyshire are among the most beautiful landscapes in the UK. The Peak District is a magnet for day trippers and holidaymakers and has been for decades. During the 19th century, newly built train lines to the High Peak brought workers from city factories wanting to escape the tough urban conditions and enjoy some fresh air as they rambled through the countryside. Along with a lunch in their backpack, the workers brought with them a frustration that much of the countryside they loved was closed off to them by wealthy landowners.

A movement began, demanding the 'right to roam', culminating in the famous Kinder Mass Trespass on an April morning in 1932. Hundreds of men and women defied the law on this historic day, hiking over restricted areas to reach the vast expanse of peaty splendour that is the plateau of Kinder Scout. Six were arrested and charged with unlawful assembly, five of them eventually being found guilty of

riot and sent to prison for up to six months. But the protest and subsequent harsh treatment of these ramblers generated a wave of sympathy for their cause and paved the way for the creation of our first national park and measures to improve access to the countryside.

Climbing up to Kinder Plateau will not make you the highest person in England. Far from it.

The 636m (2,086ft) above sea level reached at one of the plateau's three triangulation pillars makes Kinder fairly titchy compared to its bigger, bolder relations in Cumbria and even North Yorkshire. But standing on this lunar-type landscape puts you at the heart of one of the country's most significant working class protests and will also see you conquering the highest peak in our first national park. The status has protected the Derbyshire hills since 1951.

There are several routes to reach the large, flat summit of Kinder Scout, some easier than others but all of them beautiful. The simplest is a relatively flat ramble from the summit of the A57 Snake Pass, after you've done most of the climb in the car. My favourite route is from Edale, a pleasant village in the Dark Peak that has a decent-sized car park, railway station, campsites and a couple of pubs where you can celebrate your achievement with sausage and mash and a pint of local ale. Edale, of course, is the start of the famous long-distance footpath, the Pennine Way, a blissful 431km (268 mile) route that winds its way up to Kirk Yetholm in Scotland.

I've been one of the pilgrims of the Pennine Way, and there are many natural highlights to look forward to as you head north. But there's also something magical about this first day of the adventure around the heights of Kinder, setting off over farmland in the valley bottom, hiking up the paved incline known as Jacob's Ladder, and standing next to the weathered tors strewn along the southern edge of the plateau. But please choose a day when the weather is kind. Trudging up Kinder when you're getting a soaking has no element of pleasure at all.

061

SING THE WORLD'S LEAST KNOWN CHRISTMAS CAROLS

THE PUB CAROLS OF NORTH-WEST SHEFFIELD

Earliest date to take part
November 12th

Last pub sing
January 1st

Likely emotions on first visit
joy and bewilderment

Key ingredient
beer

Although supermarkets might stock mince pies from late July and some festive radio stations appear on your DAB radio in October, most people in the UK only get themselves into the Christmas spirit in December. There's a pocket of north-west Sheffield, however, where carollers sing praise to the newborn King the day after commemorating Armistice Day. Pints of beer in hand and with a wonderful community spirit, they take to a select number of Sheffield pubs and pull out their specialist book of local carols.

And then, becoming more confident with every carol and each sip of ale, they belt out a string of titles you will never have heard of unless you've been to one of these memorable events. You won't find 'Away in a Manger' or 'O Little Town of Bethlehem' here. The repertoire is more likely to contain the likes of 'Spout Cottage', 'Back Lane', 'Malin Bridge' or 'Jacob's Well'. So you'll need to shed out a few pounds for the book of carols used in the pub you find yourself in. Often the pubs have their own carol book; some hostelries sing carols never heard

anywhere outside its own four walls. You should certainly check out the events at the Crown and Glove in Stannington, The Plough in Low Bradfield and the Blue Ball in Worrall.

The experience, the carols sung, and often the tunes they are sung to, will vary from pub to pub, even though they are just a few kilometres apart. The traditions in each place have evolved over the years – and keep evolving – to make each pub sing a unique event. Some will feature brass bands, some may have a pianist. Some

may just have local ale as an accompaniment to aid the voices stood around the bar.

Despite having gained attention in national newspapers and on the TV, the tradition of the Sheffield carols remains a secret to many. I grew up in Sheffield, just outside the catchment of these fascinating pubs, and knew nothing of the local sings until my 20s. There are thousands in the city who have never heard of them to this day. But you'll also come across people who have heard about this festive musical treat and have travelled from far and wide to experience it. At the carol sings I've spoken to people who drove up from Nottingham and London. There have even been carol groups from the USA who have made the trip across the Atlantic to listen to the beer-fuelled merriment firsthand.

The precise reasons why this local tradition has survived in the pubs of north-west Sheffield, and across into north Derbyshire, have been lost over the generations. The origins seem to be wrapped up in the reluctance of 19th century churches to play jolly Christmas tunes and so the musicians and singers performed them outside and often walked around the villages as they did. Maybe one cold evening they were invited into a pub and it took off from there. Folk experts point to the working class roots of the singing and say it might just be sheer chance that it's been preserved here – in relative isolation – for so long.

However it evolved, the Sheffield carolling tradition is now a key fixture for many local folk. It's simply a joy to get involved with. Visit www.localcarols.org.uk to get an up-to-date list of the events in November and December.

062

MUNCH ON A PIE AT THE WORLD'S OLDEST FOOTBALL GROUND

Club formed
1860

Playing at Sandygate since formation

Home to
Hallam F.C. and the world's oldest football cup

Other sport played here
cricket

SANDYGATE STADIUM SHEFFIELD

Mention record-breaking English football to fans from around the world and their first thoughts might turn to large crowds at Premier League matches or perhaps the highest amount of money paid for one of the top players. Not many football fans would think of a leafy suburb in north-west Sheffield as holding a significant record in the multimillion-pound football industry.

Attending a game at Hallam F.C. is a far cry from turning up to watch a Premier League fixture at Old Trafford, Anfield, Villa Park or the Emirates Stadium. There's no lavish hospitality in private boxes at a Hallam game, no pyrotechnics before the kick-off, no long waits behind excited kids in the club superstore and no VAR to judge those important decisions, thank goodness. Neither will you be charged astronomical prices for the privilege.

A visit to Sandygate, home of 'The Countrymen', will reinvigorate your love for the beautiful game. For this is the oldest

football ground in the world and comes with a huge sense of pride in its footballing history. Small and full of tradition, taking in a game here will make you question why the non-league grounds in England's wonderfully complicated football pyramid are not bursting at the seams every Saturday afternoon. At Sandygate, you get closer to the action, walk around the side of the pitch, and enjoy some lovingly cooked and rather delicious footy scran.

Hallam F.C. have been playing at Sandygate since they were formed in 1860, making

this the longest-serving home of a football team anywhere in the world. They've got the Guinness World Records certificate to prove it hanging proudly in the entrance to their aptly named 1860 suite. And that's not the only record Hallam can claim. This is the second oldest football club to be formed. Ever. They came into being just three years after trailblazing Sheffield F.C. The leaders of these two clubs effectively drew up the first rules for the game we know today and held the first competitive games against each other. Hallam won a Sheffield-based knockout trophy in 1867 called the 'Youdan Cup'. It's officially the oldest football cup competition in the world. The actual Youdan Cup – also the oldest in the world – went missing but turned up thanks to a Scottish antiques dealer in 1997 and is now back at Sandygate once again.

As with many non-league football venues, the sense of community at Hallam is fabulous. Regular attendees feel like valued members of the club. There may not be a covered area and seats for everyone at big matches, the parking may be a nightmare, and the pitch might have a bit of a slope. But in many ways, this is the home of football, not just in England but the world over. Think on that for a minute. The multibillion-pound industry beloved across all continents and peaking every four years with the FIFA World Cup was all nurtured here in north-west Sheffield.

Elsewhere in the Steel City, so many other football records are broken that it's a wonder the city is not home to some kind of museum celebrating the sport. It was here that the world's oldest club came into existence, non-league Sheffield F.C.

063

DIVE INTO THE ABYSS AT THE WORLD'S TALLEST INDOOR BUNGEE JUMP

MAGNA SCIENCE ADVENTURE CENTRE ROTHERHAM

Steps to the top
143

Height 35m
(115ft)

Historical significance of the building
disused, record-breaking steel factory

Steelworkers once based here
10,000

Once the beating heart of South Yorkshire's thriving steel industry, the Templeborough steelworks once held its own world record as the largest electric melting shop on the planet. It's hard to overstate the economic importance of this huge industrial colossus. At its peak, over 10,000 people worked here. The official name of the steelworks was Steel, Peach and Tozer, but folk around here knew it simply as Steelos. It was the hub of the community and supported thousands of secondary jobs. But the demise of the British steel industry hit the region like a wrecking ball and the factory fell silent in 1993. Rather than flatten the site, planners approved its conversion to the Magna Science and Adventure Centre, an educational facility that also has space for business events, concerts, private parties and the odd adrenaline activity guaranteed to get your blood pumping.

The cavernous interior of this former steel giant has a very special feel. Often cold, in places dark, and always inspirational, this is now where children learn about the elements and where tourists of all ages enjoy the simple but fascinating Big Melt display on the hour every hour, which attempts the difficult task of recreating the noisy, bustling factory conditions from the 1970s. And in an unassuming corner of this huge space, you'll see brave souls launch down a lengthy zip line, descend the factory in a daring abseil and enjoy the rush of a freefall drop. But it's the fourth of these supersized treats that really captures the imagination.

Known as 'The Abyss', this former Rotherham industrial powerhouse is now home to the world's tallest indoor bungee jump. That's right, you cannot do a more extreme jump under a roof than here in South Yorkshire. Not only that, but this is also the only permanent bungee facility in the country. And the build up is quite something. With music pumping out to get the adrenaline going, you start to climb the 143 steps to the launch platform and pass by no less than seven large screens detailing the thrill you're about to experience. Dry ice floats around the surface, adding to the theatrics of this huge area.

Once you've had the safety talks, been weighed and had the gear attached, it's time to walk to the end of the platform and make the leap. For many, this is the toughest part of the whole experience. It's all down to you. Time to make

that bungee jump you always wanted to and enter the record books...

Brave bungee fans can book their adventure by heading on over to www.ukbungee.co.uk and selecting one of the dates the team are operating here in South Yorkshire. Turn up a bit early so you can be in time for the build up.

064

TAKE AFTERNOON TEA AT BRITAIN'S LARGEST STATELY HOME

WENTWORTH WOODHOUSE
SOUTH YORKSHIRE

Floor space
23,000m²
(247,569ft²)

Number of rooms 365

Garden area
87 acres
(352,077m²)

Unusual former use training teachers

The industrial town of Rotherham may not immediately spring to mind when thinking about stately homes. But it's here, on the rural fringes of this South Yorkshire steel-making settlement, where the largest country mansion can be explored. Wentworth Woodhouse is not just a big house; it's huge. Sat in 87 acres of land, this is not only a record-breaking country home but Wentworth Woodhouse also happens to be one of the finest examples of Georgian architecture. So pop along for an informative tour and enjoy an afternoon tea in the gallery while you're here. A visit to Wentworth Woodhouse will live long in your memory.

The home was built for the 1st Marquess of Rockingham around 1725, with building work continuing over four decades. Wentworth Woodhouse then passed to the Fitzwilliam family, owners of a vast estate stretching out as far as Peak District moorland. It spent time as a council-run teacher training college after World War II before having a couple of private owners in the 1980s and 1990s. Nowadays, the house is owned by the Wentworth Woodhouse

Preservation Society, an organisation with a mission focussed on the building's regeneration.

So just how big is the biggest of our stately homes? Well, over the five floors of Wentworth Woodhouse there are over 350 rooms that have a total floor space adding up to 23,000m² (247,569ft²). The best way to explore the spaces of the house open to the public is either to book onto a morning tour and be led by an

expert, or take your time to explore on your own and ask the stewards for any information you need. Only the State Rooms are open; many of the other rooms have fallen into disrepair and are not considered safe. And herein lies part of Wentworth Woodhouse's magic; this is not like a typical visit to a lavish stately home, the type you see in *Downton Abbey* and *Pride and Prejudice*.

The State Rooms open to the public are not filled with the expensive artworks and furniture you may be used to seeing in such a grand house. Rather than place unoriginal collections in it, the Preservation Society has decided to let the beauty of the unfurnished rooms speak for themselves. This is a stately home on a huge scale, but it's also one which requires an incredible amount of investment to restore. The Preservation Society has a plan

for that and initial work is underway, but it's a costly programme and your visit will help. Until complete, you get to see the face of a home that has welcomed royalty and Prime Ministers without its make-up on. After spending time in the house, grab a map and head out into the wonderful gardens, enjoying amazing displays of daffodils in March, bluebells in May, and magnolia in June. The garden is also a place to experience outdoor theatre in the summer.

Some might say it would be remiss to visit the largest of our stately homes and not enjoy the uplifting English institution that is afternoon tea. Served in the Long Gallery, with views out over the gardens and food from local suppliers, it's a gorgeous setting to treat yourself to sandwiches and cakes, washed down with a lovely cuppa. Book in and get more information at www.wentworthwoodhouse.org.uk.

065

VISIT THE WORLD'S BUSIEST POLAR BEAR ENCLOSURE

Land area 260 acres (1.05km²)

Number of animals 475

Number of species 100

Number of polar bears 8

Opened 2009

YORKSHIRE WILDLIFE PARK DONCASTER

It's a remarkable sight. The large white bulk of an impressive polar bear bounding across the landscape, making sure every other creature in the area knows who the boss is. You would be forgiven if you assumed you were on the Canadian tundra or exploring the Norwegian Arctic island of Svalbard. But no, you're actually in Doncaster. Yes, you read that correctly. Doncaster is the captive polar bear capital of the world. Here at the Yorkshire Wildlife Park in South Yorkshire, the polar bear is king. The main attraction. There are, unbelievably, eight of the magnificent northern beasts in this good-sized wildlife park. That's more than any other park, zoo or safari park in the world. Canada's Assiniboine Zoo in Winnipeg comes runner up to Doncaster, with a mere seven polar bears.

The Yorkshire Wildlife Park started out on a fairly small scale and has steadily expanded to add more animals and larger enclosures so that today it takes a whole day to fully explore. Even in its early days, the Wildlife Park was a certified world record-breaker. Back in 2010, it carried out the biggest rescue of captive lions, saving no fewer than 13 of the big cats from poor conditions in a Romanian zoo. And over the years it has added record-breaking new facilities. The sea lion enclosure called 'Point Lobos' is the largest to have been built in Europe. Leopard Heights is a facility designed for breeding leopards and is also the biggest on the continent.

Back to the polar bears, though. There are two areas designated to the eight big Arctic

predators, one holding two and the other containing six. They're kept in pairs, but the enclosures are interlocking so the bears can be mixed up and kept apart as the experts see fit. Things can get a bit agitated in the world of polar bears, it turns out, and they sometimes need time apart to cool down.

Watching the bears is sort of hypnotic, partly because you're sharing this unassuming part of South Yorkshire with these Arctic animals, whilst you can see suburban semi-detached houses in the background.

You wouldn't mess with them, of course. These bears have perhaps the most misleading appearance in the animal kingdom. While they seem loveable and you might think you could get away with stroking them, they are, of course, incredibly fierce apex predators that could easily tear you to shreds. This is why scientists heading to Svalbard need to have weapons training and carry a gun at all times; defending yourself against these creatures is a serious business in the wild. Thankfully, at Doncaster there are walls and fences and cages and all kinds of security measures to keep them at a safe distance. When visitors are on the path next to the enclosure they're actually above the bears and have a stunning elevated view of them as they sleep, shelter, bathe and wander around their territory. Book tickets for your polar bear adventure by visiting www.yorkshirewildlifepark.com.

066

TUCK IN AT THE WORLD'S BIGGEST FISH AND CHIP SHOP

Seats 500

Pier opened 1873

Length 102m (334ft)

BBC Chippy Ranking 1

PAPA'S FISH AND CHIP SHOP THE PIER, CLEETHORPES

Ask people to name their all-time favourite dish to enjoy when they're on holiday in the UK and you're going to divide the nation. Some will opt for a cream tea at a National Trust property, sipping their Earl Grey and prompting further subdivision about how to say 'scone' (it definitely rhymes with 'bone') and whether to put the jam on first or the cream (it's jam first and cream on top, obviously). A different section of society will shun the tea and scone combo and turn to the seaside, where they will partake of takeaway fish and chips, cradled in paper – or these days likely in a small cardboard box – and doused in curry sauce, while sat on a bench looking out to sea. These salt and vinegar-loving, mushy pea aficionados are my type of people, whether in Whitby or Weymouth, Blackpool or Bridlington, Skegness or St Ives.

Grimsby, of course, has a proud history of fishing and of providing much of the nation with fruits of the sea. Next door, the popular coastal town of Cleethorpes serves it up to the thousands of visitors arriving by train, coach and car. Fish and chips is more than just a snack in Cleethorpes; it's a world-beating institution. For it's here, on the town's much-loved pier, that you'll find the biggest fish and chip shop on the planet. The large white building on the short pier has been home to a number of establishments over the years, including shops, a tea room and a night club, where the fun-loving youth of Lincolnshire would dance into the night.

Today, it's much quieter but as grand as it's ever been. The large space inside is now decked out with neatly laid tables that can accommodate as many as 500 people wanting to tuck into their fish supper at Papa's. The Cleethorpes branch of Papa's opened in 2017, the latest addition to the business, which started in 1966 and is the oldest family-run group of chippies in the country. If the weather allows it, you may want to eat your fish and chips outside on the pier; there's a separate kiosk outside available for those not wanting to have waited service.

Wherever you use a metal or wooden fork to make a start on your seaside meal, you're almost certainly going to enjoy it. Papa's is not just home to the world's largest chip shop, it's also been certified as the best in the country. Competitions declaring particular chip shops to be 'the best' or 'one of the best'

are not uncommon. At any one time, there will be several chippies declaring themselves to be prize-winners worthy of note. But this particular search for 'Britain's best fish and chip shop' was a lengthy and detailed affair, taking in thousands of outlets, backed by the BBC, enjoying regular screen coverage, and involving many food experts. The upshot was that Papa's was declared to be the finest chip shop in the country, meaning the restaurant on the pier can now claim a double record-breaking accolade – it's the biggest and the best.

067

Length 2,200m
(7,217ft)

**Height of
towers** 155.54m
(510.3ft)

**Total cable
length**
70,811km
(44,000 miles)

**Depth of
foundations**
8m (26.2ft)

THE HUMBER BRIDGE NEAR HULL

When the Humber Bridge was opened by Queen Elizabeth II in July 1981, along with much media attention and a flypast by the Red Arrows, it was officially the longest single span suspension bridge in the world. With a total length of 2,200m (7,217ft), it held on to this record-breaking claim for an impressive 17 years before losing the title to a bridge in Japan. But the Humber Bridge, which shaved 96.5km (60 miles) off the distance for commuters travelling between Hull and Grimsby, remains the longest suspension bridge in the world you can walk or cycle across. So put on some sturdy footwear and bring your camera, because this walk is both a challenging and rewarding experience.

Firstly, this is not just 'a short stroll across a bridge.' A walk to the far side and back will likely take you an hour or more. Also, I'd only attempt this one if you've got a head for heights. Once you're away from the land and moving out towards the middle of the bridge, it's a long way down as you gaze at the swirling, fast-moving, tidal water below you.

The footpath and cycle lane built onto the Humber Bridge is on the west side of the

structure and is an addition many modern bridges, to their loss, don't include. There's something enormously satisfying about crossing the Humber Bridge on foot or on bike. I've done both and I enjoyed it each time. When you cross this bridge, and many others, by car, it's quite exciting seeing it for the first time and travelling along its length, but the experience is very quickly over. Being on foot or on a bike allows you to pause for thought several times as you make your way across, get up close to the cables

and towers holding the whole thing up, and enjoy the unique view afforded by the bridge, from high up above the middle of the Humber.

Every week, 120,000 vehicles cross over the bridge, paying a toll to do so. Passage for those on foot or using pedal power is free and you'll probably only be joined by a handful of other folk. For the grandeur and unique nature of this activity, there just aren't enough tourists enjoying it. San Francisco's Golden Gate Bridge is always rammed with people who've hired bikes to cycle across, with others striding over the famous span over the bay.

Now, I'm aware that Kingston-on-Hull may not have the same tourist appeal as San Francisco and that the Golden Gate Bridge has appeared in a few more films than the Humber Bridge, so has a bigger global reputation. Even so, I was surprised at how few people were taking a walk across the bridge with us. We saw a small number of tourists taking a stroll and a group of teenagers making skateboarding videos. There certainly wasn't the sense that this was a regional or national attraction. Other people are missing out, but that's no reason why you should.

It doesn't really matter which side of the river you start your journey; the aim is to get to the middle and enjoy the moment suspended above the river. The path you walk or cycle on is surprisingly wide and well-designed for the time, and there are good places to park up and explore at both the north and south sides. On the Hull side, directly under the bridge, you'll find Hessle Foreshore with a pub. On the southern side there's a visitor centre and cafe.

068

YORKSHIRE'S EAST COAST

Number of breeding seabirds
300,000

Length of coast
27.3km (17 miles)

Most common species
guillemots

Cliff rock type
chalk

Immersing yourself in the natural wonder of a thriving seabird colony is one of the most amazing wildlife experiences to enjoy on these shores. There are plenty of places to take in the joy of seeing nesting birds soaring over your head in the thousands; boat trips are available all around the British coast. But this is a book about record-breaking so we're looking for the extreme version of birding

And you'll find that on the east coast of Yorkshire between Bridlington and Flamborough, a 17-mile (27.3km) stretch that has been declared the most populous location for breeding seabirds. The roll call of birds is impressive. In the height of the summer when these cliffs are at their busiest you can expect to see puffins, guillemots, kittiwakes and more gannets diving into the deep blue ocean than anywhere else in England.

Together, there are nearly 300,000 breeding seabirds who come here and successfully fledge 113,000 young.

These are incredible numbers and some estimates put the figures even higher. This is definitely the place to come to be mesmerised by the swooping, swirling, darting patterns of courting couples heading to and from a birdopolis built vertically onto ledges on the chalk cliffs. The way the birds are able to leave the tantalisingly tiny spot on the cliff, head off to feed and then casually rock up at exactly the same point with a fishy snack is nothing short of being a wonder of nature. For a mere human, finding that same ledge among thousands of other birds is like looking for a flying needle in the metaphorical haystack.

There are two ways to experience the east Yorkshire bird colony, the first being from the clifftops at the RSPB's Bempton Cliffs visitor centre. Here you can learn heaps about the different birds and their habits, the challenges they face, and how numbers around the UK are changing. You can take a refreshing walk along clifftop paths and enjoy the view out to sea. And, when you reach the all-important clifftop, take out your binoculars to get a close-up of the puffins nesting there. As I've said already, there are many species of birds here. But let's be honest – it's all about the puffins. These unusual-looking birds are adorable as they fly in their mad-cap manner to the sea and return with a beak stuffed full of fish.

It's quite a moment seeing one up close for the first time. Expect more oohs and aahs from fellow visitors than you'd hear at a fireworks display in early November. What you can't get a feel of on the clifftop, however, is the sheer extent of how big this bird city is. It's tricky to get a perspective of how many kilometres this feeding frenzy stretches on for and to appreciate how many birds are perched on the ledges, utilising the full height of the cliffs. For that, you're gonna need a boat.

Trips leave Bridlington and head out on the waves, lasting up to three hours, to get a better perspective of the amazing bird life on the cliffs. You'll be on board the well-known Yorkshire Belle and voyages are organised by the RSPB. You need to book ahead. During May, June and July you can expect to see plenty of puffins, while August is the month to get close to diving gannets. The season comes to an end in September, when boat trips look out for masses of migrating seabirds.

069

AIM FOR A FUN DAY OUT AT THE UK'S LARGEST COLLECTION OF WEAPONRY

Number of live demos each year 1,200

Number of exhibits 8,500 on display

Total artefacts in the collection 75,000

Space 9,290m² (100,000ft²)

THE ROYAL ARMOURIES LEEDS

Anybody interested in military history will have a field day when they visit the Royal Armouries in Leeds, home to the UK's largest collection of weaponry. Saying the displays in this impressive building are vast is somewhat of an understatement. The Hall of Steel – a giant staircase allowing visitors to climb to different galleries – is alone home to 2,500 swords, spears, guns and pieces of armour. And that's before you enter the main exhibitions. The displays are arranged with pristine care and allow you to take a journey through the history of warfare. Weapons and historical documents trace how military forces have armed themselves and fought, from medieval battles right up to modern technology used in conflicts.

What sets the Royal Armouries apart from some stuffy museums that also have old weapons on display is the range of events they put on to attract families and let visitors see how good (or, in my case, bad) they are at using weaponry. One of the best activities to take part in here is the firing of a real, loaded crossbow on a special firing range. Expect a bit of a queue for this one. You'll also need to bring along steady nerves and an unwavering hand to have full control of this powerful weapon and see your bolts hit the target. You'll have eight shots and must build up a healthy number of points on the target if you're going to be one of the day's sharpest shooters.

There's also a constantly revolving number of displays for you to marvel at, many of these

involving the firing of real weapons from the past (don't worry, they use blanks!). Witness the difference between the types of guns used in the two world wars. Going further back in time, and being one of the most popular displays, guns from the Wild West are brought out and fired so you can see the sights and hear the sounds of a typical 19th century North American western gunfight. Horse shows put a range of Elizabethan equestrian skills on display, with combat demos proving how hard it was to scrap with opponents while kitted out in suits of armour. There are galleries dedicated to the history of hunting, as well as the art of self-defence. Look out for early examples of bullet-proof armour and martial arts weaponry.

The best time to make a visit to the Royal Armouries, however, is over a weekend dedicated to a jousting tournament. There are so few opportunities to witness a full-on, unchoreographed joust where competitors are really going for it. It really is something special. Admission is free to the armouries but you'll need to buy a ticket to sit in the jousting arena and it's best to do this well in advance at www. royalarmouries.org. The jousting arena will host several competitions during the event, and there's plenty of pomp and pageantry to make it all extra special. It's literally like stepping back into medieval times. You half expect Robin Hood to pop along and carry out a raid.

A day at the Royal Armouries is far more than simply wandering around looking at gleaming swords once used to injure and kill people. There is a truly interactive programme of displays and shows here, set in a building crammed full of weaponry that has seen some of the key moments in history unfold.

070

CRUISE INTO BRITAIN'S DEEPEST, LONGEST AND HIGHEST CANAL TUNNEL

Opened 1811

Length 5,189m
(3.2 miles)

**Number of
tunnels** 4

Time to build
17 years

Powered by legs

STANDEDGE
TUNNEL MARSDEN

Getting from east to west across the Pennines can still be a headache today, so you can imagine how much of a nightmare it must have been for 18th century industrialists wanting to move materials and products. Horses trotting over the hills can only move limited amounts at slow speeds, so when businesses started to hear about those newfangled waterways called canals there was a ripple of excitement in the northern air. Would it be possible to link Yorkshire in the east with Lancashire in the west, without having to traipse over those pesky hills so often daubed with foul weather?

The gauntlet was thrown down to the engineers of the day – could they build a new transpennine waterway that would be a solution to the hilly geographical problem they encountered? The answer, emphatically, was 'yes' and it became the record-breaking engineering feat you can still explore today.

At 5,189m (3.2 miles), Standedge Tunnel is the longest ever built for canal journeys on these shores. It's also the deepest, with the

hills above towering up to 194m. And with the canal being 196m above sea level, Standedge is also the highest canal tunnel in the country. This subterranean route for boats is the only one of its kind to dissect the Pennines, though other tunnels were built later when trains began ratting through the countryside.

As cars and lorries started to dominate transport in the 20th century, canals were quickly forgotten, and the tunnel fell into a

state of disrepair, eventually being closed off in 1944. Large gates were placed at either end of the tunnel to stop boats entering. And this remained the case until a regeneration project allowed people to safely enter Standedge Tunnel once again in 2001.

Today, there's a visitor centre with a café, and the towpath up to the tunnel entrance is a popular place for those walking and cycling. The towpath doesn't continue into the tunnel, though. That decision was made to cut costs when this famous route was being built. And so instead of having horses to help navigate the long, dark route, boats had to be 'legged' from one side to the other. This saw the guys on the boat lay on their backs and use their feet on the roof of the tunnel to push the vessel along. It was slow going, and with few passing places there was a limit to

the number of boats that could get through in a day.

Entering the tunnel today is like heading into a different world; it's a real window to the past. The great news is that you can do just that – boat trips regularly take curious folk into this wonder of engineering to see how goods traversed the Pennines before the steam train chugged along. You'll see just how narrow the tunnel is, discover how different sections were made from varied materials and learn about how this important route was used. Book your journey into the tunnel at www.canalrivertrust.org.uk.

071

Length 9km (5.5 miles)

Climb 295m (970ft)

Road B6138

Steepest gradient 10 per cent

CYCLE THE LONGEST CONTINUAL INCLINE IN ENGLAND

CRAGG VALE NEAR HEBDEN BRIDGE

When the Tour de France 'Grand Depart' was held in Yorkshire and the world's top cyclists sped around the county for two days, one of the most challenging sections of the route set off from Mytholmroyd, just outside Hebden Bridge. This is a settlement accustomed to challenging environments and extremes. The steep sides of the valleys in these parts can see flash floods in heavy rain, something I was reminded of on my arrival on hearing the terrifying, Cold War-style siren that echoes through the streets when flooding is imminent. Thankfully, it was just a test this time and my attention returned to the lengthy ascent leaving the village.

Turning off the A646 and following the sign for Crag Vale, the road heads past some stone cottages and starts to climb. It then climbs a little more. And continues to climb. And climb. This is officially the longest continuous incline on English road networks and with pretty views from every angle, it's easy to see why it was a favourite with organisers of le Tour. Cyclists now come here simply to have a go at the steep challenge, but also to include it as part of a much longer day ride. A sign at the start of it declares the climbing challenge is now named after local teacher Oliver Collinge, who had lived at Cragg Vale and sadly died in 2016.

The sensible cyclists among you will check the weather before attempting to complete this road-based challenge. The climb starts near the civilised setting of Hebden Bridge, a place famous for being hip, alternative and inclusive. But the

incline ends in the wilds of the Yorkshire moors, where the county gives way to Lancashire. There is a world of difference between these two places. Horizontal rain is as common on the hills as vegan food and double shot lattes are in the town. Even if there's very little wind forecast, it is likely to still be windy at the top. And with the prevailing wind being a south-westerly, you're going to get it hitting your face as you concentrate on pedal following pedal.

This isn't the hardest cycling challenge you could do; although some of the inclines are tough over a short distance, there are plenty of sections that aren't too hard work. The main problem is that it just goes on and on. Up and up. Without the occasional dips where cyclists can get their breath back. Even when it looks like the top of the hill is reached and the road can climb no more, the malevolent landscape

somehow manages to manipulate the road into climbing for another kilometre or two.

As soon as you cycle past the sign welcoming you to Calderdale, all you need is your brake to head back down to the starting point. You'll want to stop a few times, I imagine, as the dramatic moorland and valleys open up before you; it's much easier to take in the beautiful surroundings when you're freewheeling down and not busting a gut on the climb. Be sure to give a nod to the other cyclists you'll pass on your way up and down this extraordinary road; you're likely to have company when ticking off this challenge.

072

RIDE THE LONGEST ROLLER COASTER IN EUROPE

Height 65m (213ft)

Drop 62m (203ft)

Top speed 74mph

G-force 3.5

Duration 3 minutes

BLACKPOOL PLEASURE BEACH

Whoever came up with the name 'The Big One' for this monster of a roller coaster was the undisputed master of understatement. This epic and iconic ride is not simply 'big'. It's huge. Enormous. Colossal. Gargantuan. It strains your neck as you gaze up at the red and blue twisting track from the Blackpool seafront. It dwarfs the shops and houses. It may not be as symbolic as Blackpool Tower, but it's just as dominant on the town's skyline.

Entering Blackpool's Pleasure Beach is not like visiting any of our popular inland theme parks. This collection of extreme rides dates back to Victorian times, and many of them have become household names enjoyed by generation after generation. The entrance building, containing the ticket office, shop and toilets, is quickly rushed through by many a youngster keen on getting their seat on Valhalla, Steeplechase or the Flying Machines. But spare a moment to gaze around what is a beautiful Art Deco introduction to the park, and one which sets it up in a historical context.

Depending on your level of bravery and/ or craziness, queueing for The Big One will be either something you're magnetised by or terrified of. Watching the carriages make the ridiculously long climb up the impossibly steep incline, and then hearing the screams as it freefalls down towards the coastline, is not something that leaves many people sitting on the fence. But if you can build up the courage to get strapped into your seat, you're in for a treat. The anticipation and anxiety of that lengthy ascent gives way to a brief moment of enjoying the far-reaching view of the

Lancashire coastline. And then begins the rush of adrenaline as you whizz from one end of the park to the other, experiencing a menu of emotions ranging from terror to maniacal happiness. Many roller coasters are quick affairs that are over soon after they start, but not this beast. This goes on and on and on, leaving you in no doubt that you're aboard something special. It's a joy.

The Big One is a roller coaster that oozes records. When it was opened in 1994, it was the tallest roller coaster in the world, rising to a stunning 65m (203ft) from the ground. It was also the steepest on the planet, with an incline angle of 65°. It remained the tallest in the UK until Hyperia opened at Thorpe Park in 2024 and – with a track length of 1,674m (5,495 ft) – it's still the longest ride in Europe.

Pleasure Beach is record-breaking thanks to many of its other rides as well. Here you'll find the UK's largest collection of wooden roller coasters. One of them, The Grand National, is one of only three Möbius Loop roller coasters in the world, meaning that two carriages can set off at the same time on a dual circuit before returning to the opposite track. This is a brilliant, historic ride to experience, though be warned that you get thrown around on this wooden gem in a much rougher way than you do on the modern coasters. Outside another of the wooden icons, The Big Dipper, you'll see a plaque to the exploits of Richard Rodriguez, a coaster fan who set a record by spending 1,000 hours in these white-knuckle carriages during August 1998. I wouldn't recommend trying to break that one. Check opening times and book online at www.blackpoolpleasurebeach.

073

**Number of
attractions** 18

**Roller coaster
length** 250m
(820ft)

**Height of waves
in the wave pool**
1m (3ft)

**Wet weather
value** priceless

SANDCASTLE WATER PARK BLACKPOOL

The coastal extravagances of Blackpool quite rightly take up two entries in our quest for record-breaking things to do in Britain. So you've ridden the longest roller coaster and experienced the oldest rides at the Pleasure Beach. But what to do if the weather takes a turn for the worse?

Thankfully the answer lies pretty much across the road from the Pleasure Beach in the form of a water park. Sitting right on the sea front and conveniently next to the Blackpool tram, this is the place you can raise your spirits when the temperature drops and the rain falls. It looks exciting enough from the outside when you pass it on the road, all the tubes of the rides weaving their way around the building, refusing to reveal any of the mystery contained within. But once you pay for your entry ticket and pass through the doors into the tropical world beyond, that's when you can really get excited.

Here in the heart of Blackpool, a vibrant, colourful, splashtastic adventure awaits people of all ages in an environment where the temperature never dips below the mid-20s. There are 18 different rides and attractions to explore, so you're unlikely to run out of things to do. Truth be told, it's very possible you won't get around everything in your first visit. The beauty here is there's something for everyone, whether it's cascading down an adrenaline-fuelled slide and splashing into a tropical pool or simply getting afloat and enjoying the warm water while the seaside joy erupts around you.

Out of all the rides, my favourite has to be the world's first uphill water roller coaster, known as the Masterblaster. White knuckle rides are usually associated with outdoor theme parks, but this one will have you thrilled and giddy in your stomach just as much. It's the longest indoor ride of its kind in the UK, covering some 250m (820ft). Incredibly, the rafts you ride in are propelled up slopes by fast jets of water, allowing you to float down the other side, and creating the ups and downs of a traditional coaster. It's a high adrenaline ride you'll never forget, covering some seemingly impossible uphills and memorable downhills.

Elsewhere in the water park, pay a visit to Montazooma, with zoom being the operative word here. A hair-raising water slide, you'll pelt downwards head first on an adventure that takes you around hairpin turns and 360° helixes. And if that's not enough to quench your need for speed, try out the Sidewinder. This is the world's first indoor white knuckle sidewinder ride, and you're sure to hear screams and laughter as people pelt down the half-pipe course. It features an almost vertical drop, so is another of the Sandcastle rides that's not for the faint-hearted. Once you've plucked up the courage to take it on, though, I'm pretty sure you'll be back in the queue to have another go.

The sea at Blackpool is notoriously chilly, so it may be better to head for the water park's Typhoon Lagoon if you want to experience some soothing waters and exciting waves. The wave pool here can produce breakers 1m (3ft) tall, and the pattern they hit you with varies. There's a lot of fun to be had inside this Sandcastle (www.sandcastle-waterpark.co.uk).

074

DESCEND THE TALLEST UNINTERRUPTED WATERFALL IN THE UK

GAPING GILL
YORKSHIRE
DALES

Height of waterfall
100m (328ft)

Length of main chamber 129m (423ft)

Height of chamber
31m (101ft)

Chances to descend each year 2

It's one of the most spectacular natural features and thrilling experiences the nation has to offer, and yet when you arrive here it looks like there's nothing here. Standing at the side of Gaping Gill, you might wonder what all the fuss is about. The 90-minute walk across the Yorkshire Dales from the small village of Clapham is pleasant enough, heading past some show caves and taking in some inspiring northern scenery. But when you arrive at Gaping Gill, it's just a fenced off hole in the ground.

Despite looking unremarkable on the surface, the beauty of this fabled Yorkshire spot is in what lies beneath. When the babbling waters of Fell Beck have meandered down from the source to reach this point, they tumble down into the abyss and become what is Britain's tallest waterfall. The problem is, you normally can't see it. In fact, to get up close with Gaping Gill's torrent of cascading water you really need to become a bit of a daredevil.

Unless you're a confident caver with lots of experience potholing in the Yorkshire Dales,

don't even think about attempting this on your own. But thankfully there are two weekends every year when you can explore this record-breaking waterfall with guides, during a couple Bank Holiday weekends in May and August. Over the three days of those extended weekends, this remote hillside turns into a camp made up of cavers from clubs at Bradford and Craven. They set up a structure across the hole leading into Gaping Gill and winch people down one by one into the vast subterranean space beneath your feet. Taking one person down and then bringing one person back up the 100m

(328ft) drop is a time-consuming process so expect a little wait. It may be that you book in, pay the charitable donation and get given a rough time you can expect to be called for your adventure.

When it is your moment to sit in the small chair and be lowered into the ground, you're in for such a treat. Strapped in and seeing the horizon disappear, your journey follows the vertical drop of the waterfall and it's common to get the odd splash from the spray as you descend. Although you're suspended in mid-air with feet dangling, it's anything but scary. In fact, it's one of the most beautiful experiences I've ever had. You have time to look around and fully take in your surroundings, seeing the tall, narrow plume of water cascade into the gigantic cavern emerging around you on all sides.

At the bottom, you'll spend the first few minutes craning your neck to gawp at this incredible space. The sound of the water crashing on the rock is naturally harsh, yet gently therapeutic. The light shining through the rock at the top of the waterfall is sublime. The head torches of the potholers emerging from the darkness after making their own way down the labyrinth of routes is surreal. Gaping Gill is part of a long and complex cave system that links with Ingleborough Cave. The first descent here was made by a local man named John Birbeck, who was lowered on a rope by farm workers in 1842. He reached a point 58m (190ft) down that's still known as Birbeck's Ledge. It was Frenchman Edouard Martel who first touched the floor of the main chamber in 1895 using a rope ladder and a candle. Thankfully, there's not as much effort involved for you to make your own journey.

075

First audiences
1788
___

Capacity 214
___

Good place for
plays, music,
stand-up
___

Panto? Oh, yes,
there is!
___

WATCH A SHOW IN BRITAIN'S OLDEST UNCHANGED THEATRE

GEORGIAN THEATRE ROYAL RICHMOND

Whether you want to watch a string quartet or get a little bit shouty at a pantomime, enjoying a night at the theatre can be a transformative experience creating, long-lasting memories for young and old. Sometimes, on entering a theatre you've not been in before, your breath can be taken away simply by gazing upwards at the historic surroundings, imagining the hundreds of shows that have been performed there over the years, and the famous people treading the boards.

So where are the record-breaking theatres in the UK? The West End, you might think. And you would be right in many cases. The site of the Theatre Royal Drury Lane has been entertaining crowds since 1663, including early audience members King Charles II and Samuel Pepys. But that theatre has had more than one guise. To step inside the oldest working theatre still operating in its original building, you need to venture a long way north of the West End to the small market town of Richmond in North Yorkshire. Here, on the edge of the Yorkshire

Dales where the beautiful River Swale has carved out a stunning valley, you will discover the Georgian Theatre Royal. Enjoy a production here and you'll be stepping back in time to 1788 when the doors were first opened to audiences seeking entertainment.

Built by local actor Samuel Butler, the theatre was a popular addition to the town and reflected the growing demand for entertainment here and in the surrounding rural villages. It was initially part of a circuit of theatres built in northern

towns such as Beverley, Harrogate, Whitby and Kendal. This is the last of those venues to remain open. The Georgian architecture you'll see in this historic theatre is typical of the classical style of the day, with a symmetrical façade and tall sash windows. Inside, there's ornate plasterwork, pillars and the traditional u-shaped seating arrangement. You really are offered a glimpse into the theatrical world of the past.

Check out the theatre's website (www. georgiantheatreroyal.co.uk) to discover what performances are planned. It's always good to experience this amazing and historic space in the way it was intended – by seeing a play, or perhaps an opera. The town has a great reputation for staging pantomimes every year, so making room in your calendar for a Christmas visit will provide a healthy dollop of festive cheer.

But if the 'What's On' listings don't tickle your fancy, make sure you book in for one of the theatre tours. The guided trip around this historic building will allow you to delve deeper into the secrets contained in the nooks and crannies of Richmond's Royal Georgian Theatre. Dressing rooms, backstage areas, and the stage itself, are all places you'll visit, hearing stories of actors, special performances, stagehands and architectural features along the way. One of the highlights is another record-breaker; the theatre is home to the oldest surviving stage scenery in the world. The Woodland Scene dates back to around 1820.

076

Length 18km
(11.23 miles)

Area 3,632 acres
(14.7km²)

Max depth
67m (219ft)

**Number of
islands** 19

WINDERMERE
CUMBRIA

For many, the ultimate Cumbrian experience is hiking up a fell to take in the solitude, fresh air and 360° views. But there's an equally serene opportunity if you head out onto one of the many lakes this district is named after. Visitors can launch on the water for free at such iconic locations as Ennerdale and Derwent Water. But if you're wanting the record-breaking Lakeland experience, there's only one stretch of water to head for – Windermere.

Of the many Lake District ribbon lakes created when Ice Age glaciers carved and scraped out the landscape we are familiar with today, the longest is the long, thin, bending, bony finger that is Windermere. Measured from the northern shore near Ambleside to the southern access point at Fell Foot Park, Windermere clocks up 18km (11.23 miles). It makes it the longest lake in England, and for good measure, it's also the record-breaker in terms of area and volume of water. There's only one thing to do: take a kayak from one end to the other!

I'll freely admit that I decided to do this challenge without giving much thought as to how hard it would be. I'm not an Olympian and the kayaks we were using weren't the highest quality. As a result of these factors, the going was generally slow and the whole trip took close to five hours. Of course, you may give yourself a different kind of challenge out there on England's longest lake. Perhaps you'll aim to paddle around one of the islands or tackle the width of Windermere. It's not necessarily about going from end to record-breaking end.

Getting out onto this stretch of water for any activity will get you up close to this watery record holder.

One of the trickiest decisions is where to enter the water. Most of the Windermere shoreline is privately owned and you're not allowed to launch any vessel from there. But public jetties are available and the website of the Lake District National Park (www.lakedistrict.gov.uk) has all the intel on where they are. If you're not carrying your own kayak, there are several places around the water's edge where you can hire one for half and full days, and you can launch from there, too.

For the super adventurous, there is an unofficial challenge to kayak along the threesome of long lakes in the region – Windermere, Ullswater and Coniston Water.

I set off with oar in hand to tick off all three, but started with Windermere to get the hardest one out of the way first. An end to end Windermere kayak will take a moderate amount of planning before you get in the water, primarily because you will end up just over 11 miles away from where you started. Two cars would be ideal, or at least a working knowledge of the local bus timetable.

Turning around and paddling back is not recommended and is a solution only for the super human. The best advice has to do with your direction of travel. This is a north to south trip because that is the way the water steadily flows as it enters into the River Leven at the southern end and slips away to Morecambe Bay. If you're going to paddle your way along the longest lake in England, you may as well have the current on your side.

077

Summit 978m
(3,209ft)

Home to highest
tarn in England

Climb time
around 6 hours

Formed over
450 million years
ago

HIKE TO THE SUMMIT OF ENGLAND'S
HIGHEST MOUNTAIN

SCAFELL PIKE
LAKE DISTRICT

Hiking to the top of all the Wainwrights in the English Lake District is on the bucket list of many energetic hill walkers. The collection of 214 peaks is named after famous outdoor author, Alfred Wainwright, who compiled a now legendary seven-volume walking guide, complete with detailed drawings and incredibly neat, handwritten notes. These books can now be bought alongside tick lists, wall charts and scratch maps – all showing your progress over the years as you near your end goal of joining the 214 Club.

And, yes, such a club does exist. The members on this exclusive list are able to buy badges, t-shirts and certificates to show off their achievements. The challenge of walking the Wainwrights and reaching the summits of the nation's most famous mountains is to be savoured rather than rushed. There are guides out there that suggest you can complete the Wainwrights in just over a month, if you're built like Captain America and don't need to work or rest. Realistically, this is a task to be enjoyed over many years with several friends. Savour

it. And perhaps give yourself an extra reward when you reach the peak of England's highest mountain – Scafell Pike.

Although tackling this mountain should, in theory, be easier than walking to the top of its loftier cousins Ben Nevis and Yr Wyddfa, don't be fooled. Like all the highest Lake District fells, this is going to provide you with a demanding day's activity. You're going to need maps, a good pair of boots and walking gear. You'll probably be aching the day after and in no fit state to climb

more Wainwrights on consecutive days. But is it worth it? Goodness me, yes it is.

But, whatever you do, head to the correct summit. There are two peaks up there, fairly close to one another. One is called Sca Fell and is 964m (3,162ft) above sea level. The one you're after is Scafell Pike at 978m (3,209ft) above sea level; you'll know the difference because there's a trig point at this one and it'll be where all the people are having selfies. You don't want to make all this effort and realise you stood on the wrong peak.

There are three main routes to get to the summit. They're all beautiful walks and they all lead to England's highest mountain, but they have different lengths and challenges so it's worth checking out your preferences before you set off. The shortest, most direct route is from Wasdale, a stunning valley you approach from the western edge of the national park. The view of Scafell from the valley bottom was voted Britain's favourite view, and you'll also pass Wastwater, a gorgeous lake that holds the record for being the deepest in England. With great paths to follow, this is perhaps the best one if it's your first time.

Whichever way you decide to walk up to the top of Scafell Pike, plan to do it on a day when the weather is on your side. That way, you'll get treated to the view. Standing as the highest person in England, you can look out to sea beyond Wasdale and the Cumbrian coast. You'll also be able to survey the majestic 360° horizon of other Lake District fells. You may even have caught the bug and plan which ones you are going to do next... Plan your hike at www. scafellpike.org.uk.

078

DRAW A PICTURE AT THE HOME OF THE WORLD'S LARGEST COLOURING PENCIL

DERWENT PENCIL MUSEUM KESWICK

Length 7.91m (26ft)

Made 2001

Weight 446kg (983lbs)

Colour yellow

With glorious fells rising all around the town and a lake to go out boating, there's little that can get in the way of a good time in Keswick. Except, perhaps, the weather. The Lake District is well known for being the wettest place in England and many a well-intentioned holiday has been hindered by horizontal rain and howling gales. You're going to need a wet weather plan (or two) in the Lake District, and thankfully there is a record-breaking museum that will put a smile on your face. The Derwent Pencil Museum is centrally located and a firm favourite among regular visitors to Keswick.

So why is it here? Well, Keswick is literally the home of pencils. Graphite was discovered in the Lakeland valleys centuries ago and the world's first writing pencil was assembled here. The town was home to a busy pencil factory from 1832 until 2007, when production moved to nearby Workington. And now, it's home to two enormous pencils – both of which do actually work! The key feature is the biggest colouring pencil in the world, a huge and very heavy yellow item measuring close to 8m (26ft) long.

You can also have your photo taken next to a massive writing pencil, which is the biggest in the UK.

Despite being a relatively low-key museum with an unusual subject matter, the Pencil Museum in Keswick is packed with fascinating exhibits. Alongside a detailed history of pencil making, lots of interesting pencil memorabilia can be found. Small pencil sculptures are a curious feature on the shelves, and a commemorative

pencil for the Diamond Jubilee of Queen Elizabeth II is here, too.

But I'm a geography teacher and there's one exhibit I found especially fascinating. Pilots flying daring raids over Germany during World War II faced many risks, one of them being stranded in a hostile nation in the event of crash landing. And in that frightening circumstance, those RAF personnel could turn to their trusty pencils. On getting the innocent-looking writing implement out of their jacket, they could snap it in half to find a small map of the country inside. It all sounds very much like a James Bond story, but these were used in the war and would point the servicemen in the right direction to plan their escape back to Blighty.

It's not going to take you a long time to go around the exhibits at the Pencil Museum. But

for the artistic souls among you, this visit could turn into a much lengthier affair once you leave the displays and head into the café area. Here, while ordering a coffee and a bite to eat, you can take part in some therapeutic pencil sketching or, if you're like me and can't draw for toffee, you can do some good old colouring in. Like I said, I am a geography teacher.

The museum is on the site of the former Derwent Pencil factory, which made pencils here in Keswick for decades. Although the pencils are now made elsewhere, the brand still exists and they are high quality, as you'll discover when you put graphite to paper. You can, of course, take a selection home from the museum shop. There's no need to book in advance for the museum. More information can be found at www.derwentart.com.

079

WITNESS ENGLAND'S OLDEST RED DEER RUT

Herd here for
300 years

Weight of a male red deer 190kg (418lbs)

When to go
October and November

Best time
sunset

MARTINDALE
CUMBRIA

Every autumn, the amazing sights and sounds of rutting deer fill a remote Lakeland valley with wonder. Although rutting deer can be seen in many estate parklands across the country, there's definitely something special about making the trip to Martindale, where you'll find England's oldest herd in healthy numbers. The rut, the deers' mating season, happens over several weeks, with stags fully focused on warning off male rivals and attracting female mates. During this testosterone-fuelled time, a large stag can produce its loudest calls, perform better in duals, and so may have up to 40 mates in its harem.

The first time I heard the rutting of the red deer in this fantastically remote and beautiful valley was quite by accident. I honestly had no idea that here in the northern reaches of the Lake District was a herd of red deer that has wandered these hills for centuries. I was setting off on a walk to tick off a couple of Wainwrights and enjoy the blue skies of a clear autumnal day. My hiking obsession had made sure I went up the hill known as 'The Nab' and a couple of others along the way, but it was the

sounds, rather than the views, that grabbed my attention on this particular walk. Because I wasn't expecting to come across the deer, I found the noises almost incomprehensible at first.

My brain was telling me it had to be sheep on the fells, but it clearly wasn't. It just didn't make sense. Could it be a dog? No, the sound was coming from all around us, up on the hills and down in the valley. After a few minutes

of listening to the deep, captivating calls, we spotted something moving way down below us in the valley. Although it was a long way off and appeared tiny, you could just about make out the well-camouflaged deer strolling among the foliage. Spending time nearby so many of the nation's largest land animals is genuinely something to behold.

Once you spot one of the grand creatures down in the valley bottom, it seems to get easier to pick out dozens more as you become aware of the scale of your surroundings and can identify the colour of the deer. Pressing further on up the hill, not all our encounters remained at a long distance. As the valley disappeared behind us and the path arrived at the fell tops, the calls continued and groups of deer appeared much closer. As the route rounded corners and brought new areas into view, we got fairly close

to red deer on several occasions and could sit down to observe their behaviour. Once they became aware of us – either through seeing or smelling us – they were out of there instantly. But the moments we gained beforehand were extra special.

As wild animal encounters go in Britain, this is among one of the most majestic and elusive. And despite being in a remote Cumbrian valley, it's within an easy drive from many British cities. You'll find Martindale close to the northern shores of Ullswater; pass through Howtown and drive as far as you can, making sure you only park in designated areas. Once on the walk, you should keep at least 50m (164ft) from the deer (keep in mind the extra hormones pumping around their body during the rut), so taking binoculars might enhance your trip.

080

DRINK A BEER IN ENGLAND'S HIGHEST PUB

Height above sea level 528m (1,732 ft)

Previous name Kings Pitt Inn

Windows let no draught in

THE TAN HILL INN
MUKER

At the northernmost tip of the Yorkshire Dales National Park, flanked by the Pennine Way and with no neighbours as far as the eye can see, Britain's highest pub is as welcoming as it is legendary. The Tan Hill Inn stands 528m (1,732ft) above sea level and commands great views in every direction. It's a great place to take in a countryside walk and be sure that there'll be a good meal and an array of ales awaiting your return.

As well as the many daytime visitors, the Tan Hill Inn is a very popular nightspot, despite its remoteness. The lack of light pollution means it's a great place for stargazing on clear, dark winter nights. Strike it lucky and you may see the northern lights from here. Rooms are available if you want to make an overnight stay of it, while the hilltop location has become something of a cult destination for campervan owners who pay a charity donation to stay in the car park. A good programme of cover bands and the occasional comedy night means it's always a popular weekend haunt.

People sitting outside the Tan Hill Inn on a summer evening, enjoying a pint while bands take to the outdoor stage, might check their surroundings and ask what on earth a public house is doing here in the first place. It isn't here to serve any community, at least not one that is apparent today. But once upon a time there was a working coal pit nearby. Miner's cottages sprung up in the surrounding fields and the inn was a vital hub for them to socialise in. The Kings Pit Inn, as it was then called, took its name from the coal mine that operated until 1929.

Although the houses and workings have long since disappeared, the Tan Hill Inn has survived – largely thanks to effective management in getting folk to make the trek here. The Tan Hill Inn was the first pub where you could get married and it's featured as a location in TV shows such as *Vera*. Allowing campers and putting on entertainment has ensured people are prepared to venture into the middle of nowhere to enjoy a drink at the highest altitude possible in the UK.

There's often a gale blowing outside, so it may not surprise you to learn this is the pub where Ted Moult tried to sell you Everest windows by dropping a feather to prove their draught-free reputation. The feather used to be framed in the bar until it was half-inched by some underhanded visitor. The winter months bring plenty of extreme weather to these parts.

On more than one occasion, drinkers have been snowed in up here and had to wait days for the roads to be cleared. There are worse places to be stranded.

Head into the lounge and you'll see there, on the wall, a Guinness World Record certificate proving this to be the highest pub in Britain. This was once a bone of contention, with the Cat and Fiddle near Macclesfield also claiming the distinction. But official measurements gave the prize to the Tan Hill Inn – winning by just over 12m (or 42ft)! Today there's a whole host of merch you can take back with you to prove you have spent time in the nation's highest pub.

081

THE ANGEL OF THE NORTH GATESHEAD

Completed
1998

Weight
208 tonnes
(458,562lbs)

Height
20m (65ft)

Wingspan
54m (177ft)

Angel's favourite footballer
Alan Shearer

For those with roots on the Tyne, nothing says, 'Welcome home!' like the Angel of the North. At the end of a long drive north to Gateshead and Newcastle, the winged figure rises high above the trees and beckons you on for the last few kilometres. We all have landmarks near our home telling us we're nearing the end of the journey, but this has to be one of the finest.

The tallest sculpture in England and the biggest depiction of an angel on the planet, Anthony Gormley's rusty coloured, heavenly messenger has become one of the nation's biggest icons. Seen by an estimated 33 million people every year as they drive by on the A1 and A167, the angel's remarkable size and elevated position on a hill gives it a considerable vantage point. But rather than just motoring past and perhaps raising a smile at this northern angel, follow the brown signs and pay her a visit. You can park up here and head into the grounds where the angel has been installed, with foundations so deep that it is able to withstand winds stronger than 100mph. There's no rope or barrier to keep you away from this public piece of art. You can stand by the plinth and pose for family pictures, although you'll need to stand a long way back or have amazing photography kit to get the whole of this immense sculpture into your shot.

The Angel of the North has become more popular with people in the North East over the years, but it certainly divided opinion when it first made an appearance back in 1998. Some loved it, some loathed it. But a prank by some

Newcastle United fans helped to turn the tide in its favour. To mark the arrival of striker Alan Shearer at the club, the Angel of the North was seen on the news wearing the black and white shirt of the Magpies' new number 9. It raised the profile of Gormley's work to a different level entirely.

Looking up at the north's angel, the wings stretch out further than a Boeing 767 and look mesmerising as the clouds float by above. Each of those wings weighs in at 50 tonnes (110,231lbs) and together make up half of the sculpture's 208 tonne (458,562lbs) total. It's as tall as a five-storey building and there's enough steel up there to make 16 double decker buses. As well as reaching 20m (65ft) high, the foundations for the angel also reach 20 metres into the ground; huge concrete piles anchor Gormley's masterpiece to the bedrock deep

within the hill. The Angel of the North was a remarkable achievement, costing £800,000 in the late 1990s.

Just how much the Angel of the North has been taken to heart by people in the region can be seen in the touching tributes to loved ones that have been left nearby. Flowers, messages and mementos have been left in a dedicated memorial garden towards the bottom of the hill. This is a site occupied by an angel, after all. The Angel of the North is not just the tallest sculpture in England, it's also become a giant symbol of remembrance, love and spirituality.

082

First Hoppings fair 1882

Rides 400+

Length of fair 1km (3,280ft)

Tallest ride 60.9m (200ft)

ENJOY THE THRILLS OF EUROPE'S LARGEST FUNFAIR

HOPPINGS FUNFAIR NEWCASTLE

Lasting for just over a week every June, Hoppings Funfair puts Newcastle on the global thrill-seeker map. Attracting much media attention across the north of England every summer, this showcase of travelling excitement rolls into town and pulls in over 400,000 visitors. On an even bigger scale than the Hull Fair and Nottingham's Goose Fair, this gargantuan gathering of rides and attractions is a family-friendly explosion of the senses. The sights, smells and sounds make it a must for many folk in the North East and an integral part of a Geordie summer.

The diverse range of activities on offer at this extravaganza mean you can spend your time on anything from the toddler-favourite hook-a-duck through to white knuckle thrills. You can be turned upside down, spun around and propelled at high speed if that's the fun you're looking for, or you can head for the dodgems, take the kids to the bouncy castle, or try a few less demanding roller coasters. End to end, the Hoppings site is 1km (3,280ft) long, and as darkness falls it turns into a Vegas-style glow of neon.

And, of course, a travelling fairground has a very different feel to a permanent theme park. For a start, the expectations are lower, largely because getting inside doesn't break the bank. But often the excitement is higher when you go to a city-based fair that is not always there. At a theme park, you know it's there all the time and you know exactly what you're going to get. But a travelling fair? Well, these guys come into your neighbourhood, bringing mystery and intrigue. Things can be a little more edgy, and

the sides less polished. And it's only here for a limited time. So throw caution to the wind, get out there and enjoy the rides, the candy floss and the games where you could win a giant, stuffed Minion. Throw the darts to win a prize, see if your stomach can stand the drop tower, strap yourself in and endure the spins and somersaults. Head home with a bucketful of adrenaline, and come back tomorrow to make the most of the opportunity before the trucks roll away to the next town.

The fair's location has a centuries-long history of hosting celebratory gatherings. Travelling fairs have taken place on the Town Moor in Newcastle since the 13th century. The Lammas Fair was one of the originals, and several others were held throughout medieval times at Whitsuntide. 'Hoppings' was a term in the North East for feasting, dancing and general merry-making. Perhaps contrary to this ancient tradition of indulgent fairs, The Hoppings funfair started life much later in 1882 as a Temperance Fair, promoting the abstinence of alcoholic drinks.

Once again held on the Town Moor, the current incarnation of the Hoppings is a continuation of the travelling fair tradition. It is the stuff of legend, looked forward to by hundreds of thousands of revelling folk from the North East, all looking for a good time in the summer evenings. The history of The Hoppings matches its grandness, creating a temporary event that is the envy of thrill-seekers across Europe. Entry is free, with payment needed for the rides and attractions inside. Get excited at www.hoppingsfunfairs.com.

083

Population 3,811

Distance from Hadrian's Wall
3.2km (2 miles)

Myth busted
it's not named after a railway stop

Record contested by
Dunsop Bridge, Lancashire, and a few others

HALTWHISTLE
NORTHUMBERLAND

Exactly where do you have to stand to be at the centre of Britain? Is it one of the capital cities? Is it the furthest point from the sea? Or should we treat the question more as a metaphorical one? Maybe we should not be asking about a physical place and instead searching for the events and activities that are closest to the beating heart of the nation. For some, being close to the centre of Britain might mean having a cream tea in Devon. For others, it may involve taking part in a Burns Night Supper or going to see a Shakespeare play in Stratford.

But as well as the country having many cultural centres, it's possible to stand right in the geographical 'middle' of Britain. This will be easy to find, you might think; just draw lines from all four corners of Britain and the point where they cross will be the centre.

Well, when you look into this you learn very quickly that it's not so simple. The first issue to deal with is whether you're looking at just the island of Britain or do you want to extend it to

Northern Ireland and Ireland? And when you consider that Britain is a three-dimensional land mass positioned on a sphere, it turns out that finding the exact centre is fairly tricky.

And then there are the tides to consider. Do you make the calculation at a sandy low tide or at high tide, when there is much less land exposed? So, when you look into it, declaring one place to be the undisputed middle of Britain can be quite a nightmare. There is one settlement, though,

that has done more than others to declare itself to be at the heart of the country.

Welcome to Haltwhistle! On entering this small Northumberland town, you'll be left in no doubt you're in a place of utmost importance. This is the 'Centre of Britain', the middle of the country. And there are large signs to prove it. Haltwhistle is a very pleasant market town, with a smattering of decent shops and a secondary claim to fame that it's the closest community to Hadrian's Wall, just a few kilometres away. You can visit the remains of the castle and if you want to stay overnight, there's the Centre of Britain hotel. That's right, a hotel named after the geographical accolade. So, it must be true. Right?

The way the good people of Haltwhistle have worked it out is as follows: find the line of longitude which covers the most land in Britain and locate the midway point along it. And there you'll find the town of Haltwhistle. Other places certainly disagree. Take Dunsop Bridge in Lancashire, for example. A complex investigation by The Ordnance Survey to find the gravitational centre of Great Britain laid the trophy at their feet. The geographic centre of the United Kingdom is somewhere in the middle of Morecambe Bay, which is not too useful. If you're after the place furthest from the sea it's at Coton in the Elms, Derbyshire. The point furthest away from a high tide centre mark – including rivers – is just to the south-west of Lichfield.

084

WALK ALONGSIDE BRITAIN'S LONGEST WALL

HADRIAN'S WALL

Length 117km (73 miles)

Overall height 4.5m (14.7ft)

Width Up to 3m (9.8ft)

Length of walking trail 136km (84 miles)

It's one of our oldest historical sites. A world-famous landmark. Up here, in the wilds of Northern England and close to the border with Scotland, Hadrian's Wall is one of the best destinations in the UK to enjoy a real sense of history and imagine the events that took place centuries ago. The wall was, of course, built under the command of Emperor Hadrian. He was a leader who travelled extensively throughout his Roman Empire and invested a lot of time overseeing border defences. And so this incredibly ambitious plan was unveiled to keep the folk north of the wall out of the empire. When the Romans arrived in Britain, it was a place of warring tribes and some were involved in rebellions against the invaders. To keep them at bay, this huge structure was built and occupied by Roman soldiers who came from as far away as Romania, North Africa, and what is now Syria.

Spanning 117km (73 miles) and made of local stone, this thick defensive structure is so much more than just a wall. Along its route there was also an earthwork, a ditch, three bridges, 16 forts, 80 milecastles and 160 turrets. An incredible achievement, taking 1,080 working days to add every 100m (328ft). And every one of those 100m sections of wall contained an astronomical 2,352 tonnes (5.2 million lbs) of clay and stone, such were the dimensions of a wall that was up to 3m (9.8ft) thick and over 4m (13ft) high. Today, the wall isn't visible all the way along its path across northern England, but there are sections where the fabulous ruins are available to explore.

Unsurprisingly, the most visited spot on this historic, record-breaking wall is the best preserved at Housesteads Roman Fort. A short walk up the hill from the visitor centre takes you to a well-presented museum and then into the ruins of the community that lived and worked here. From this point, you can go for a stroll alongside the wall and soon get to the Sycamore Gap, the point where the famous 'Robin Hood' tree stood until it was illegally hacked down in 2023.

Chesters Roman Fort is another location with jaw-dropping ruins and artefacts, this time all centred around a bathhouse that was well used by those stationed here at the northern extremity of the empire. And in Vindolanda there's another chance to get up close to some of the Roman discoveries made locally. The museum here is a delight, and there are still some excavations ongoing.

It's best to visit in spring or summer when the visitor hours and the daylight are on your side. That way you can pack more Roman action into your time here, discovering how Britain's longest ever wall helped to bring stability to this empire outpost. And if you're feeling like a real cool adventure, you can walk the length of the wall, from the appropriately-named Wallsend to Bowness on Solway. Along the way you'll get up close to the remains of this magnificent structure, seeing how it adapted to the landscape to include hills and cliffs. The views are also epic.

085

BE BRAVE AND STEP INSIDE THE UK'S DEADLIEST GARDEN

THE POISON GARDEN ALNWICK

Number of poisonous species
150

Number of annual visitors
600,000

Largest garden area 42 acres
(169,968m²)

Plants you can touch NONE!

It's not the biggest garden in the UK, but the perfectly presented and tellingly fenced off Poison Garden at Alnwick has more than enough toxins to do you some serious damage. This is the deadliest collection of plants in the country – so keep your hands to yourself and do as you're told!

There's nothing in this little garden area that isn't dangerous. The 150 species of plants here haven't been selected for being pretty and having lovely flowers. The gardeners are more concerned with plants that could be used for dark means; they're toxic, intoxicating and narcotic. Entry to the Poison Garden is included with your ticket to Alnwick Gardens and this is but a small area of what is a fantastically renovated attraction. But make sure you go in there on one of the official tours that set off every 30 minutes; you'll learn so much and hear a wealth of fascinating tales about these incredible plant species.

Sitting next to Alnwick Castle, the gardens were first laid in 1750 under the guidance of the 1st Duke of Northumberland. Seeds were brought from all over the world and the gardens at Alnwick soon developed a reputation for their grandeur and topiary. The estate suffered due to the austerity of the 20th century, however, and by the 1950s the garden had all but been abandoned and fallen into disrepair. A major regeneration programme was kickstarted in 1997 and visitors to the first phase of the new Alnwick Gardens were welcomed in 2001, with extra zones being opened up in the following years.

There's lots to enjoy and take in when you visit these magnificent gardens, including water features, a treehouse, bluebell woods, and superb flowerbeds. But from the moment it was unveiled in 2005, the Poison Garden became a major attraction here and word quickly spread about the excellent tours. The idea for this rather dark but fascinating specialist garden came from the Duchess of Northumberland herself, and she played an active role in overseeing the garden's re-emergence as a regionally important visitor attraction. It's now one of the USPs of Alnwick Gardens and the reason many curious visitors come, whether or not they're into gardening. Or poisoning, for that matter.

It's quite an exciting step to go through the metal gates emblazoned with a skull and crossbones, with the words 'Can Kill' beneath

them. Expect a safety briefing before the tour starts. Many of the species here can be grown anywhere in the UK, with some needing more specialist care. The most poisonous plant, according to the Guinness World Records, is the castor oil plant, and of course you'll find that here. There's a laburnum tree, the second most poisonous tree in the UK; a dog chewing a fallen stick from this tree can fall seriously ill. Rhododendrons contain a poison that can be very harmful to humans and stop other plants from growing nearby; if bees make honey solely from Rhododendron flowers, it can make you hallucinate, while larger doses can kill you.

There are dozens of other deadly stories to listen to in the UK's deadliest garden, including that of how a bush manages to release cyanide gas and can be potentially fatal for gardeners. Plan your visit at www.alnwickgarden.com.

086

CYCLE AROUND THE LARGEST MAN-MADE LAKE IN NORTHERN EUROPE

KIELDER RESERVOIR
NORTHUMBERLAND

Litres stored
200 billion (439 million gallons)

Length 9km (5.65 miles)

Width 3.2km (2 miles)

Max depth 52m (170ft)

Holding a staggering 200 billion litres (439 million gallons) of water, this huge body of water in Northumberland is easily the largest reservoir in the UK by capacity. Better than that, it's the biggest man-made lake in Northern Europe. In a truly remote setting, the Kielder Reservoir is surrounded by the huge Kielder Forest, which itself is one of the biggest man-made woodlands in Europe. You get the feeling here that you're in the middle of nowhere. And that's because you are.

The plans to construct this monster of a reservoir were first drawn up in the 1960s at a time when the rising population and development of industry in the UK meant there was an extensive thirst for more fresh water. Work eventually began in 1975 and the dam wall was completed in 1981, and officially opened by Queen Elizabeth II. The nation had seen nothing like it before, and it at once started to make a real difference to those in charge of water supply in the north of England.

To give you an idea of just how big Kielder Reservoir is, the perimeter of the shoreline measures in at over 41.8km (26 miles). It's pretty much a marathon in the woods. And on one weekend in the summer, it does actually become the route of a marathon, with runners tackling the off-road route with all of its gentle undulations as it circumnavigates the water. The track that hosts the energetic marathon competitors, as well as shorter running challenges, too, is a key component of the area's massive recreational value. Rather than

simply leaving the reservoir off-limits, as so many are, the designers incorporated a track around the edge of the water and encouraged tourists to flood in to get to know this once-ignored corner of the country. It provides a much-needed economic boost to the small communities in the area and allows visitors to leave refreshed and invigorated. At least, that is, when they don't have to endure a week of rain and wind here. I've been there and done that. It leaves you soggy and questioning your life choices, but hopefully you won't have to endure this existential crisis of a holiday and will have a nice time instead.

The path around the edge of the water is the perfect place for a day's walking or an afternoon bicycle ride. And so, on a warm, summer's day, expect the place to be busy with hikers and cyclists enjoying fresh air and the stunning views. For although this is a man-made landscape, and some would say a purpose-built dam and coniferous forest is a sterile environment, I think the skyline up here is outstanding. There's a spiritual benefit that comes from being next to the water, and the unfurling evergreen forest makes you feel like you're in Canada or Scandinavia. The main centre to find information and get hold of a snack is found at Kielder Village.

As well as giving you a feel-good boost, this destination is also good for the environment. Kielder Reservoir is home to the biggest hydro-electric power plant in the country, making an important contribution to reducing carbon emissions.

087

STARGAZE BENEATH BRITAIN'S MOST PRISTINE DARK SKIES

Opened 2008

Designated International Dark Sky Park 2013

Number of stars visible billions

Experience rating out of this world

KIELDER OBSERVATORY NORTHUMBERLAND

Anybody who watched *The Sky at Night* as a kid or got lost in an astronomy book knows the wonder involved when you gaze up at a clear sky away from the orange hue of city streetlights. Getting into the countryside away from built up areas is so important for stargazing; the more remote you are, the better it gets. Across the United Kingdom, there are no fewer than six national parks that boast International Dark Sky Reserve Status because of their distance from the light pollution of towns and cities. But there is only one location that has been designated an International Dark Sky Park, and that's Northumberland. The skies above Northern England are officially the darkest in the country and it's the second largest such site in Europe. There are several sites within this astronomically significant boundary that are fantastic places to spend a chilly evening staring upwards. You just need to keep your fingers crossed for a clear sky.

If you'd like to stargaze across the Dark Sky Park that is Northumberland, perhaps the best place to head for is the Kielder Observatory, dramatically set atop Black Fell in the middle of Kielder Forest. Established in 2008, the aim of this fabulous building was to produce a few dozen events a year for members of the public, but huge demand for their space-themed talks and tours soon ensured a rapid expansion. Today, the experts at the observatory hold more than 700 talks, and most of them sell out in advance, so booking ahead is essential (www. kielderobservatory.org).

The most popular events are the Aurora Nights. These evenings explore the beauty of the northern lights, cover the science behind them and explore the best places in the UK to spot them. The intriguing night also includes a tour of the observatory's facilities and a chance to meet the team of astronomers based there. Whether or not you get to see any stars or planets, of course, depends on the weather, but here's hoping you pick a good night for your visit.

Although the information and experience you gain at the observatory is not to be missed, there are also spots you can head for a free evening beneath the stars. Wrap up warm, pack your torches and head to Cawfields, a rocky location close to one of the best stretches of Hadrian's Wall. It's near Milecastle 42 and the jagged crags of Whin Sill, where you're far

enough away from the bright lights to enjoy a smashing view of the stars.

Being in this dark sky zone on a clear night is a thing of wonder; don't think you're just going to look at a few stars. As many as 85 per cent of people living in the UK have never experienced this kind of dark sky, and never seen the stars in the way they can be seen. On a clear night here, the sky is lit up with the light from billions of stars. We're talking about skies so dark that – incredibly – it's possible for the Milky Way and the planet Jupiter to cast shadows in the middle of the night.

088

HIKE ALONG BRITAIN'S TOUGHEST NATIONAL TRAIL

Established
1965

Length 431km
(268 miles)

Highest point
Cross Fell

**National Parks
encountered** 3

Fastest time
61 hours 34
minutes

THE PENNINE WAY EDALE TO KIRK YETHOLM

A series of dramatic, challenging hills forming the backbone of the nation, the Pennines have long been the playground for the adventurous hiker wanting freedom and fresh air. Things became altogether more serious for the Pennine walker in 1965 when a formal route from Edale in Derbyshire to Scotland's Kirk Yetholm was drawn out and made into a national trail. The Pennines suddenly offered something more exciting and adventurous than a day out in the Dales.

The real kudos to be had in this range of hills was dished out to those completing the Pennine Way. With the White Peak in sight at Edale, the path heads over the peaty, desolate moorland of the Dark Peak, down into the grassy dales of North Yorkshire, through the limestone landscapes of the Yorkshire Dales, through bleak, beautiful Northumberland and over the border into sublime Scotland. With Kinder Scout, Bleaklow, Pen-y-Ghent, mighty Cross Fell, and Cheviot to be ticked off along the way, this is no Sunday stroll in the park. You're likely to encounter days of rain, misery, wet socks, blisters and aching legs before completing the tricky 431km (268 mile) route.

According to Paddy Dillon, author of Cicerone's comprehensive guide to walking the Pennine Way, this is the most challenging national trail in the country. So what finer way is there to spend a summer than by donning your walking boots, and stepping out on a project that will take you at least two weeks and give you a warm, glowing sense of achievement when you finish.

I can speak with authority on this topic, having completed the Pennine Way with my family in late 2021. We made the last steps into the Border Hotel in Kirk Yetholm just before they stopped serving food as dusk set in. The pub, like the Travellers' Rest in Edale, is the official start/finish of the Pennine Way and offers certificates for those who have completed the Pennine pilgrimage.

Getting stuck into sausages and a beer as a reward for hard work was a key highlight of the many years I've spent hiking in Northern England. But here's a confession: I didn't complete the Pennine Way in one continuous journey. It was done on weekends, a day here and two days there. Legendary fell walker Alfred Wainwright reckons that's OK, though. In his definitive book on the journey, he says it's perfectly acceptable to do it in different

sections. He even suggests it adds to the experience by making the trail last longer, giving you more trips to look forward to. So with his seal of approval, I felt like I had truly earned my sausages, beer and certificate.

Then follows the awkward decision about which direction to walk the Pennine Way. I started in Edale and headed north. Poet Laureate Simon Armitage took on the challenge heading south. I saw plenty of people mid-Pennine Way and they were tackling it in a variety of ways. Some were doing some sections heading north and others going in one journey south. I guess it doesn't matter, because the main aim of this extraordinary route is to have fun. Do the Pennine Way in any direction you wish, taking as many days as you need, over whatever time period works for you. This national trail is a national treasure.

089

BE INSPIRED BY THE WORLD'S LARGEST ARTS FESTIVAL

EDINBURGH FRINGE

Number of shows 3,500

Number of performances 52,000

Number of countries artists travel from 70+

Number of venues 200+

For a three-week period every August, Edinburgh undergoes a remarkable transformation, which sees it become the centre of the artistic world and welcome throngs of comedy, drama, cabaret and musical fans.

Hotels charging dubious prices are rammed full, keen amateur thespians hand out flyers for their new shows, public spaces are filled with bars and street food, and culture vultures compare notes on the latest five-star performances. The whole city is buzzing with excitement as thousands of performers arrive, hoping their show will be the talk of the festival, one of the sell-out acts. Some of them will be world famous, others will be completely unknown. A few will make their name in showbiz. Most will go back home out of pocket, still waiting for their big break. For the performers, the Ed Fringe can be a life-changing experience, or a harsh one (or both). But for the punters, it's usually a hoot.

Whether you come to Edinburgh during the Fringe for a day, stay overnight, or base yourself here for its entirety, the best thing you can do is throw yourself into festival spirit. How long you can do this for will depend on your budget; with tickets often costing upwards of £14 a show and hotels charging a premium rate, expenses can soon add up. But while the bank account allows, you're not going to get bored here.

There are literally thousands of shows to choose from, staged at over 200 venues. As soon as the audience for one event leaves, the waiting crowd for the next turn is ushered in. It's like a cultural rotisserie. And while

it's the comedy shows that get much of the press attention, the beauty of the Fringe is that you'll get the opportunity to see plenty of niche performances you'd struggle to experience elsewhere. Children's shows, puppetry, storytelling, magicians, dance, and bubble art. It all has its place in a staggeringly comprehensive and diverse programme.

So with all these thousands of shows to choose from, how on earth do you go about formulating your own Edinburgh Fringe experience? Well, you could browse through the website (www.edfringe.com) and see what titles take your fancy. You might find political comedies, names you recognise, or the reworking of a favourite book. Taking a punt comes with its risks though, and there are many acts that simply don't live up to their hype.

Ideally, you'll have a few friends who have been to the festival just before you and they can recommend some crackers they've been to see. If not, get hold of *The Scotsman* every morning and leaf through the extended review section, making a note of who got the four and five star verdicts. Failing that, position yourself in the Courtyard at The Pleasance for the afternoon and get chatting to fellow festival goers to see what they have enjoyed.

I find the Edinburgh Fringe to be so eclectic, so different every year, that I quickly became addicted to it. Having visited the city during the festival by accident over 20 years ago, I've been back most years and have passed the hunger for it onto my children. I generally go for two or three nights, but could happily stay for the full three weeks. And when I leave, I tend to feel forlorn and have a longing to go back.

090

STEP ABOARD THE NATION'S LONGEST-SERVING ROYAL YACHT

Years of service
43

Length 126m
(413ft)

Height 37m
(121ft)

Capacity 250
guests

Number of crew
21 officers and
250 Royal
Yachtsmen

ROYAL YACHT BRITANNIA EDINBURGH

Since the restoration of Charles II as monarch in 1660, there have been no less than 83 royal yachts used to entertain dignitaries, provide private space for the royal family, and transport kings and queens around the world. Charles II himself loved a royal yacht; he had 25 of them on the go. But none of the royal vessels lasted as long or covered as much distance as HMY *Britannia*. In a naval career that lasted 43 years, *Britannia* visited over 600 ports in 135 countries, clocking up over a million nautical miles (1.6 million km) of travel – the equivalent of going all the way around the world every year of her service. The Royal Yacht *Britannia* has entertained celebrities during formal dinners and played host to several American Presidents and British Prime Ministers. It's well and truly a record-breaking royal boat.

Times change, though, and we found ourselves in an era when air travel is more convenient and beady eyes are rightly scrutinising how every penny of public money is spent. Whereas once a monarch could have argued the case for having multiple royal yachts, today the building of a new floating palace would seem lavish and wasteful. And so, when the Royal

Yacht *Britannia* was decommissioned in 1997, it became the final vessel of its kind and that chapter of royal history was closed. When Queen Elizabeth II left the yacht for the final time, all the clocks on board were stopped and to this day show the time she alighted – 3.01pm.

Today, HMY *Britannia* is seen by thousands of people every year, but not as she rides the waves and charms foreign diplomats; this time people travel to her as she sits resting in the dock. Following decommissioning, interested cities were invited to submit bids showing how the *Britannia* could be used as a catalyst for urban renewal. Edinburgh's plan to breathe new life into the Port of Leith and Ocean Terminal developments won the day and so the Royal Yacht *Britannia* has become one of the most popular attractions in the Scottish capital.

The Ocean Terminal shopping mall and car park building would be unremarkable at best were it not for the entrance to the royal yacht being built into its upper level. But when you pass through the gates and board the yacht, you enter a world of decadence that gives a solid insight into aspects of royal work and

life. Of most interest are the royal sleeping quarters (separate rooms for Queen and King with an adjoining door), the studies used for correspondence, and the large dining room used to host foreign leaders.

It's not all glitz and glamour, of course. The lower decks are home to the far more cramped living conditions of the crew and military band that accompanied the royal party. The immaculately polished engine rooms are also of note, as is the huge laundry room where uniforms would be cleaned and pressed. Sometimes crew members had to wear several different uniforms in one day to meet the royal requirements. This insight into the royals at sea is like none other available in the country. It's a little like visiting a National Trust stately home that floats and used to circumnavigate the globe. See: royalyachtbritannia.co.uk.

091

Opened 1853

Power source
natural light

Best experienced
on sunny days

**Chances of
standing up in
the Vortex**
slim

TRY TO BELIEVE YOUR EYES AT
SCOTLAND'S OLDEST TOURIST
ATTRACTION

CAMERA OBSCURA
EDINBURGH

**Tourists shopping on the Royal Mile for a special tartan or a peaty dram of whisky can
be seen live on a specially built screen atop a historic Edinburgh building, the Outlook
Tower. But the moving images you can see are not being captured by the latest surveillance
technology. Oh no, not one bit. In a dark chamber sits the Camera Obscura, a circular
screen in the middle of the room that has the mystery and magic of a Harry Potter film set.**

Open to visitors since Victorian days, and using
centuries-old technology, there's no electricity
needed to get the camera working. No flat
screen HD technology, no wires connecting
everything together. The Camera Obscura –
the oldest purpose-built tourist attraction in
Scotland – uses only natural light and mirrors to
project the live images of life on the surrounding
streets and has done so since it opened in 1853.
As a result, you can expect to get a clearer
picture of what's going on outside when the
weather is bright and sunny. Dark, drizzly
weather with restricted visibility is not the friend

of the Camera Obscura, though on these days
you can see a recording of what it's like when
the sun's out.

The camera is found on the top floor of this
exquisite Outlook Tower, next to Edinburgh
Castle. From other vantage points in the
Scottish capital, you can pick out the Camera
Obscura thanks to the recognisable white
tower housing its mirrors. When you reach
the top of the building, head into the camera
room and listen to a short talk explaining how
the technology works. Then you get to gaze

upon the jaw-dropping 360° views the camera projects. This principal attraction is certainly a key talking point in the hour or two you'll spend in here, as are the views you'll get to see from the rooftop. But there's so much more to this curious visitor attraction than the Camera Obscura itself; it's also home to a 'World of Illusions'.

As you head on a one-way route up and down the stairs at the Camera Obscura, you'll discover a fascinating room full of intrigue on every floor. The emphasis here is on illusions, and there are so many little optical wonders to discover that you'll have a real job giving them all the time they deserve. Spooky holograms transform innocent-looking children into horror movie fodder as you move by them. A large 'magic eye' invites you to stare deeply into it until animals are revealed. Get lost inside a

mirror maze that leaves you questioning the reality in front of you. And stand in a cleverly created room of slopes and manipulated lines that will make two people of equal height seem like Gandalf next to a hobbit.

But when it comes to the biggest and most disorientating illusion of your entire Edinburgh experience, nothing comes close to a small tunnel of crafted carnage known as 'The Vortex'. You'd think it would be fairly straightforward to walk across a metal bridge the length of an estate car. But the swirling cylinder of lights encircling the walkway creates a masterful illusion that could very well knock you off your feet. Just to be clear – there's nothing physically moving here.

092

TAKE A RIDE IN THE WORLD'S ONLY ROTATING BOAT LIFT

THE FALKIRK WHEEL

Number of locks replaced 11

Number of annual visitors 500,000

Weight 1,800 tonnes (3.9 million lbs)

Opened 2002

Height boats are lifted 35m (114ft)

Engineers in central Scotland came up with a record-breaking, unique solution when faced with the problem of linking up two important canals. The Forth and Clyde Canal was once connected to the Union Canal by a series of 11 locks, but these had long since fallen into disrepair and, to be honest, took an age to navigate. Enter the Falkirk Wheel. One of the most distinctive and innovative feats of engineering in the modern world, this rotating boat lift makes easy work of the 35m (114ft) gap between the two waterways. The two canals had been separated since the 1930s as the original lock system was unusable, but now boats are linking up between them again and you can take a ride on it to experience the full engineering magic of a lift found nowhere else in the world.

Of course, the Falkirk Wheel is much more than a lift that connects two canals that used to have a dead end. This engineering masterpiece is a symbol of Scotland's ingenuity, and a reminder of the nation's rich cultural heritage. And it's now a major tourist attraction. Since opening, visitors have come here from around the world to marvel at the way it effortlessly lifts boats into the air and connects them to the next canal on their journey. The visitor centre brings people up to speed with the physics behind the technology, and the boat experience sees tourists getting on the boat on one canal before being lifted to the other, as if in the hand of some friendly, metal giant.

An industrial game changer that has made sure the large canals are once again linking east Scotland with the west, the Falkirk Wheel has also become a symbol for this region of Scotland, appearing in countless media articles, featuring on TV shows, and becoming a postcard pin-up to rival the nearby Kelpies. The genius of the design also ensures very little power is needed – even to move big vessels. The two gondolas involved in the rotation are always balanced due to the Archimedes Principle that the boats will disperse their own weight in water. So even if one of the gondolas contains several boats, the weight will be the same. And that means only a modest amount of power is needed to transfer boats from one canal to the other – about the same needed to boil 8 kettles. So as well as being an iconic structure with a global reputation, this is also an extremely energy-efficient structure.

Riding the Falkirk Wheel is probably the most unique and unusual boat journey in the world. There's simply nothing else like it. Anywhere. As your boat enters the lower gondola, you'll feel a real sense of anticipation and wonderment about what is going to happen. Gates close behind you, and then in almost silence and with fabulously smooth movement, the wheel starts to rotate. It's like you are magically floating in the air. Over the few minutes the ride takes, take advantage of the views; the Scottish countryside in these parts is magnificent. Once you're at the top, the boat effortlessly glides out onto the Union Canal. What a journey, certainly faster and more fun than dealing with dozens of lochs!

093

Height 30m
(98ft)

Completed 2013

Designed by
Andy Scott

Weight 600
tonnes (1.3
million lbs)

STEP INSIDE THE BIGGEST SCULPTURE IN THE UK

THE KELPIES
FALKIRK

According to Scottish legend, kelpies are cunning water spirits that take the form of horses and lure innocent victims from the safety of the land into the watery depths below the surface. There's no need to worry about any ill-intentioned goings-on from the majestic Falkirk Kelpies, though. The most likely outcome of a trip to see these two colossal statues is that you're lured into the depths of Scottish culture and want to learn more about their origin, as well as about the canal besides which they rise.

These two equine giants next to the M9 have been keeping an eye on folk in Falkirk since 2013, and have seen millions come to admire them. Easily the biggest sculpture in the UK, the Kelpies are also the largest horse sculptures in the world. No other horse's head comes anywhere near matching the magnificent and slightly menacing Falkirk Kelpies. On a clear day, you'll be able to see the reflection of these giant beasts in the Forth and Clyde Canal, which sits next to them. Boats sailing past to the west will, within a few kilometres, be at

the Falkirk Wheel, another unique and record-breaking feature along this inspiring waterway.

The main attraction in a new parkland called 'The Helix', Falkirk's Kelpies are easily explored and it's free to do so. Approaching the horses and wandering between them, their stationary heads seem to come to life as you look at them from different angles and the light shimmers off their stainless steel surface. Photo opportunities abound. But for the ultimate experience here in Falkirk, you need to book onto one of the tours.

This will answer all the questions you have about this phenomenal, world-famous work and give you much more information besides.

Sculptor Andy Scott was influenced by local industry and culture as he started the design and slowly saw his vision become both a reality and a key landmark. As well as learning about the short history of the Kelpies, you'll get a chance to become one of the few visitors who actually get to journey inside the sculpture. Yes, the guided tour is not only about appreciating these animals from the outside, but standing within the necks and gazing up from the inside of the art piece.

Reviews of the Kelpies were largely favourable at the time they were introduced, but not everybody was a fan. Over time, though, they've become a symbol of Central Scotland and a welcoming beacon for those heading north to the Highlands and south to the capital. They're so elegant, it's hard to imagine each of these graceful pieces weighing 300 tonnes (661,386lbs).

If you get a chance, visit in the day but return in the evening. After dusk, the Kelpies are lit up and sparkle different colours, giving them a totally different feel. If anything, seeing these beauties at night is a more mystical and satisfying experience. Just don't go too near the edge of the canal. We don't want these mythical creatures to lure you in.

094

CLIMB THE HIGHEST MOUNTAIN IN BRITAIN

Elevation
1,345m (4,412ft)

Number of annual visitors
130,000

Time to allow
8 hours

First climbed
1771

Average winter temperature
−5°C

BEN NEVIS
SCOTLAND

This is the big one. Hill walkers from around the world come to the Highlands of Scotland to tackle what is the biggest mountain in Britain. From people obsessively ticking off the list of Munros north of the border, to daytripping tourists on a hiking challenge from Fort William, a trek to the top and back takes most people between six and eight hours. At the top you'll find stunning views of the Highlands and an abandoned observatory that collected weather data between 1883 and 1904 and now stands lonely among a landscape of barren rock. From a distance, the distinct dome of Ben Nevis is highly recognisable and looks fairly ominous, a giant for you to scale. Some say it looks like a volcano, and with good reason; the dome of Ben Nevis was indeed part of a volcano that collapsed and is now extinct.

Ben Nevis is a mountain that needs treating with respect, though, both to protect the spectacular local environment and to keep yourself safe. Ben Nevis is not a peak you can simply set off to conquer without putting in preparation and planning. Rocking up on a random day wearing canvas shoes and a T-shirt could lead to a disastrous day for you – and a busy one for the local mountain rescue team.

Most people will set out to climb Ben Nevis in the summer months when the ice and snow at the summit have melted.

Unless you have plenty of experience with ice picks, crampons and endurance events, don't even think about tackling this beast of a mountain during the winter. Even in the height of summer, on what was forecast to be an

idyllic day, I've had to turn back halfway along the ascent because wind and rain pounded in, making the route ridiculously unsafe. There are days, albeit pretty few and far between, that you'll be able to enjoy a clear, sunny climb to the top of this fabulous peak, enjoying the far-reaching views afforded from the top. Grab hold of them when you can!

There's one main route to the top and the vast majority of walkers set off along this, leaving from the visitor centre on what is a very challenging 16km (ten mile) round trip. Even the most experienced walker should be meticulously prepared for this one, having proper footwear, clothing, plenty of water, snacks and maps. Nobody is immune to having an accident on Ben Nevis and serious incidents take place every year. So don't read the suggested kit list and think, 'Oh, they don't

really mean it, especially about the compass and map.' They do mean it.

The path to the summit is reasonably straightforward to follow in good weather when you can see it, but this is an area with a spectacularly dramatic microclimate; thick mist and fog can set in unexpectedly and leave even the most experienced walker hopelessly disorientated. Relying on your phone is not a great idea as they can pack up in cold conditions and, of course, lose battery power and service. Call in at the visitor centre beforehand to check out the weather forecast and if there are any other unforeseen problems with the route. But don't be put off by all the warnings. If you prepare well, this will be a memorable achievement that you will rightly be proud of.

095

BECOME THE STONE SKIMMING CHAMPION OF THE WORLD

EASDALE ISLAND
SCOTLAND

Maximum diameter of competing stone
7.6cm (3 inches)

Number of bounces needed
at least 2

Number of competitors skimming stones
350

Amount of practice needed
lots

We've all done it, either as a carefree child or a nostalgic adult. Standing on the shores of a lake or reservoir, picking up the flattest stone you can find and attempting to show off your silky skills by skimming it across the water. In my head before the throw, I'm always going to send the perfectly formed stone in a majestic, spinning trajectory across the water, touching the surface a good seven or eight times like a Barnes Wallis bouncing bomb. In reality, I might manage two, maybe three, bounces before it sinks to the bed of the lake a few metres from the shore.

Skimming, it turns out, is a lot harder than it seems. And explaining it to young children is even harder. The magic is all in the flick of the wrist, the creation of spin, the angle you fire it off and the speed it goes. When you get all the ingredients bang on, releasing the stone and seeing it bounce along the surface is indeed a magical experience. Not so magical is when it all goes wrong and plops into the water just in front of you. But who knows? If you brush up on your skimming skills you could end up officially the best in the world!

The annual event on the Scottish island of Easdale takes place in a disused slate quarry now filled with water. Held here since 1997, the stones used to skim in this world title fight have been worn and smoothed by the sea, making them ideal for the job in hand. Anyone can enter the Easdale competition, but don't leave it too late. The number of entrants is limited to 350. This is not because the organisers are being exclusive or mean, but simply due to the restrictions of time. They have to make sure

there is enough to get all the entrants through, and 350 is about as many as one day will allow. Even if you don't get onto the entry sheet, there will still be space for spectators so you can still be part of stone skimming history. The competition takes place in early September but check the website www.stoneskimming.com for entry requirements from March.

The rules are tough, though. This isn't something you can simply turn up and win. Some practice is going to be needed. For a start, the rock you use is crucial; you can only use naturally formed Easdale slate with a maximum diameter of 3 inches (7.6cm). If you do get a chance to be a contestant in this in-demand competition, you're going to have to get your best shot away in three attempts as there's no way you'll be allowed any more, either as an individual competitor or as part of a team. Three attempts max.

There are ropes that designate the area of play and any stones skimming out of the zone will be disqualified. Your skim will also need to bounce at least twice to be counted as a valid skim, and it's the stone that travels the longest distance that is judged to be the winner. There are rule differences to skimming competitions held in the USA. At Easdale it's all about the distance the stone travels while skimming, but in the USA judges instead look out for the number of bounces. It's competitive business. I'd very much encourage you to get involved, but I'd also advise you to spend some time at your local lake getting to your own skimming epiphany just before making the journey to this delightful Scottish island.

096

LAND ON THE WORLD'S ONLY TIDAL RUNWAY

Elevation sea level

Number of annual passengers 13,102 (2022)

Number of aircraft journeys 1,456

Surface sand

BARRA AIRPORT WESTERN ISLES

This is maybe not one for nervous fliers, or those who really want to make sure there's a solid runway beneath the plane for take-off and landing. But aircraft are designed to land on different surfaces. There are those that can safely touchdown on water, and others where a perfectly safe landing can be achieved on ice. At Barra, a small island in the Outer Hebrides, the plane has to make sure the tide is out when it lands. Yes, this is the world's only sandy runway; the only airport where the timetable has to take account of the ebb and flow of the sea.

With a population of 1,174 and no direct ferry link to mainland Scotland, the community on Barra has a strong connection with the air service. It provides a fast and regular link with Glasgow, helping islanders to reach the biggest city in Scotland and also bringing supplies and visitors back to Barra. Travellers arriving on the island do so on a Twin Otter aircraft holding just 18 passengers. As well as the sandy landing, pilots will often find the Barra flight to be a challenge because of the wind, which can be notoriously

strong up here on the Western Isles. To allow for this, there are three runways laid out on the beach, each one covered up by the sea at high tide but permanently marked by a wooden pole at one end. The strength and direction of the wind dictates which of these are used.

The airport can be found on the northernmost tip of the island at a lovely spot called Traigh Mòr. It's basically a wide bay that offers some shelter and also the all-important beach that

makes the air connections possible. Taxis can take you there and it's also a popular place for beach lovers and cockle pickers to spend their afternoons, though take note of whether the windsock is there because that'll let you know if there's a chance of the Twin Otter coming in from the mainland.

The approach to Barra's beach airport has often been voted one the best in the world, and on more than one occasion this unique and scenic location has been used as the setting of a romantic marriage proposal. With the help of airport staff and the occasional firefighter, messages have been written large in the sand to ask for a passenger's hand in marriage. On board, the lucky lover is asked to gaze out of the window, and down there on the beach they'll see their partner pop the question. For most passengers, arriving at the world-famous Barra airport does not have such long-term implications for their personal life, but the incredible views and the surreal feeling of stepping onto a sandy runway is a special travel memory that will stay with you for a very long time.

097

LAUNCH YOUR WAY AROUND BRITAIN'S HIGHEST DISC GOLF COURSE

GLENCOE MOUNTAIN SCOTLAND

Number of holes
9

Length 2.4km
(1.5 miles)

**Height above
sea level** 725m
(2,378ft)

Mountain
Meall a' Bhuiridh

**Chances of
finishing under
par** pants

It's all about throwing a disc down a fairway as accurately and quickly as possible, landing it into a basket, just like a golfer's dream of planting the ball into a hole in a small number of shots. Disc golf has been around since the 1960s but is really starting to take off in Europe, with a number of new courses being developed, some high-profile competitions taking place, and a growing list of registered players. Check out YouTube and you'll see just how skilful and accurate the professionals are, but this is something that players of all abilities can join in and enjoy.

Despite the increasing popularity of the sport, there are a lot of people who are still to learn about the joys of disc golf – or frisbee golf, as some call it. I first came across it in Mariehamn, the small capital city of Finnish Åland, which is home to the biggest disc golf park in the world and has hosted open tournaments. Our host was a teenager called Alfred, who gave us three different discs (a driver, a 'mid-range' and a putter) before demonstrating just how it's done. Needless to

say, I was rubbish compared to the locals who head out with their disc golf kit regularly. But it didn't matter, for this was a whole lot of fun.

It works in the same way that golf does; most courses are laid out over 9 or 18 holes and are given a par rating for the number of throws you're supposed to be able to finish it in. Just like in real golf, this should be disregarded as totally unachievable unless you've invested a lengthy time in improving your frisbee

skills. I went into the experience expecting to finish considerably over par and I was not disappointed. The 'holes' might be as long as 200m (565ft) so you really have to start off from the tee with a sturdy throw and hope it doesn't veer off to the left or right into woods, rocky ground, water, or 'the rough'. The nearer you get, change discs to make a shorter throw and you'll soon (hopefully) find yourself close to the basket. The final shot should be considerably easier to make than in golf; aim the frisbee at the basket and if you're in the right zone the chains will stop it so it can fall calmly into the holder. And that's disc golf in a nutshell.

And so to Glencoe, that beautifully awesome and atmospheric valley in the Highlands where you will find the highest disc golf course in the United Kingdom – and it's one of the most inspiring to boot. With the summit of this lofty course being some 725m (2,378ft) above sea level, you can hike up Meall a' Bhuiridh's footpaths to play the game, but it's going to be quicker and easier to take the chairlift. If you have your own discs then feel free to take them along. Otherwise, you can hire them at the top before you tee off.

And don't feel like you need to book in advance to play this lovely mountain course; you can turn up and enjoy the facilities whenever you like. But stick to the summer months because the course tends to be covered in snow during the shorter, colder days, which makes finding the holes significantly harder. If you do get the bug for playing disc golf having thrown your frisbee way up here, there are a growing number of courses around the country.

098

Height 15m
(50ft)

Width 40m
(130ft)

**Number of
annual visitors**
40,000

**Chance of seeing
a dragon** slim
these days, but
you never know

VENTURE INSIDE BRITAIN'S LARGEST SEA CAVE ENTRANCE

SMOO CAVE SCOTLAND

It can feel like you've reached the end of the earth when you get to the northernmost coast of Scotland. After all, you could take a boat in a straight line from here to the north pole and not hit any land. Staring out across the vastness of the Atlantic Ocean evokes all kinds of adventurous emotions. This is a magical place where stories conjure up a land of myths, legends and fantasies. If dragons were real, there'd certainly be one that lived here. By day, it would sit atop cliffs and gaze out to the misty northern waters. By night, the giant creature would retreat to protect its hoard of gold inside the largest sea cave entrance in the country. Smoo Cave evokes such fantastical thoughts, and it's wrapped up in history and folklore.

Your visit will likely start from the car park, signposted from the nearby main A838 road. From here, you need to climb down a set of wooden steps and it's during this descent when the extent of the cave becomes apparent. It's massive. Deep, wide and tall. And as well as winning the plaudits for being the biggest sea cave entrance on the mainland, it's clearly

one of the most spectacular ones as well. The reason for its photo-friendly dramatic appearance is down to the Allt Smoo stream that cascades from the surface into the heart of the cave from a sinkhole that collapsed and opened up this subterranean gem to the surface. This hole allows natural light to flood into the cave as well as the torrent of water,

giving a clear view of an underground stream that would otherwise be in darkness.

Boat trips into this incredible space, a wonderful coincidence of nature, are unforgettable. You get off the boat at the other side of the cave and can walk along a narrow ledge to get up close to the cascading gem at the heart of Smoo Cave. You'll also learn heaps about the cave's geology, history and erosion, bringing you right up to date with how this very special landform was created.

So what's the best time to make your visit to the record-breaking Smoo Cave? Well, it depends on the type of experience you are looking for. The boat tours are only available in the summer months, when the weather is milder. But these are times when the crowds are there, too; many of the 40,000 annual visitors rock up in July and August. If you're looking for a quieter experience, time your trip to be away from the school holidays and avoid the summer. An off-peak experience will give you more time to admire the cave and take memorable pictures, though you can expect the weather to be chilly and there won't be any boat trips available. Up here, on the north coast of Scotland, you're in for one of nature's biggest treats no matter what time of year you arrive.

099

STAND ON THE NORTHERNMOST POINT OF MAINLAND BRITAIN

CAPE WRATH
SCOTLAND

Lighthouse built
1828

Latitude
58.62°N

Max cliff height
281m (921ft)

Area 68,448
acres (277km²)

**Length of track
from ferry**
17.7km (11 miles)

Most people head to John O'Groats when searching for the northernmost extreme of Britain. But the coachloads of tourists looking for their selfies with the sign pointing to Land's End are very much in the wrong place. You can see why John O'Groats has become the go-to northern extremity. It's the sort of the north-western extreme that could be seen as pretty much the furthest point away from Land's End in the south-west. It's also close to the road and ideal for daytrippers. But it's definitely not the northernmost point of Britain. That compass record-breaker is found at the formidable-sounding Cape Wrath, a rugged clifftop destination in the extreme north-west of the nation, often pounded by stormy seas and strong winds.

Getting to Cape Wrath is not the most straightforward of journeys by any stretch of the imagination. It's 193km (120 miles) further north than Inverness, which itself can be a slog to reach. There's no 'Cape Wrath train station' or direct bus service connecting it to the nearest Scottish town of Durness. You can't even take your own car there, and that is one of the attractions of this northern beauty.

To make the pilgrimage to this fantastically isolated spot and stand where only the most adventurous manage to reach, you need to arrive in tiny Keoldale and get the passenger ferry across the Kyle of Durness. At the other side, a minibus takes intrepid travellers along the 17.7km (11 mile) rough track north to this Scottish extremity. This bumpy journey can be slow-going and takes about an hour, but the

driver will be cramming your head full of local knowledge as you creep along. Space is limited to get you there, so you'll have to reserve a space if you want to spend three hours at Cape Wrath and then return to get the ferry back on the same day. See www.visitcapewrath.com for everything you could wish to know about arranging your journey.

A lengthy challenge though it is, standing on the cliffs at Cape Wrath is reward enough – providing you're not battered by howling winds and intense rain. But on a fine day, the picture-postcard lighthouse and biggest cliffs in Britain conjure up the rare treat of a remote coastal paradise. The place is teeming with bird life, with gannets, rock pipits, cormorants and golden eagles being common sights in the air.

On the land, look out for sheep grazing and the odd red deer gracefully standing on the horizon. Wild waves smash onto jagged rocks at the bottom of cliffs made of sandstone and metamorphic rock as you carefully peer over the abyss. In what will come as a relief to many, life on the edge also has the oasis of the Ozone Café. It's a welcome refuge on days when the weather is not on your side – both for a cuppa and the chance to warm up.

100

Scheduled flight time 90 seconds

Fastest time 53 seconds

Distance 2.7km (1.7 miles)

First flight 1967

FASTEN YOUR SEATBELTS FOR THE WORLD'S SHORTEST COMMERCIAL FLIGHT

WESTRAY AIRPORT ORKNEY

Many travellers completing a long-haul flight to some far-flung corner of the world know the frustration of watching a couple of films before realising there's still six hours until they land. That's not a problem for the people of Westray, Orkney, who fly to visit their friends on the neighbouring island of Papa Westray. These travelling Orcadians won't even have time to get to grips with the in-flight magazine before it's time to get their baggage down from the overhead lockers. Sat on the runway on Westray, you can pop a boiled sweet in your mouth just as the plane taxis to the runway, but you're unlikely to have finished it before the pilot begins their descent and the wheels touch down on Papa Westray.

And that's it. That's the flight. Finished without the obligatory nap or the gander at the hospitality trolley. It usually takes around one minute to complete, compared to the 25 minutes it takes on the passenger ferry between these two communities. The flying schedule links the two islands in the north with Orkney's main settlement, Kirkwall, in a triangular route. And it won't break the bank, either. The short passenger flight can be booked for less than

a tenner, although you do have to get up to Westray first to enjoy it.

Orkney is a beautiful holiday destination, packed with architectural wonders of global importance. Some of the significant finds on the islands predate the pyramids in Egypt, yet have less fuss surrounding them in terms of visitor numbers and information centres because of their remote location. But if you have a read

of any comprehensive guide to these islands you'll also find mention of the world's shortest passenger flight, not as a handy transport tip but as a tourist attraction. And so the aircraft, which has just ten seats available, is often sold out and there are many holidaymakers who have made this journey. But the route has also proved crucial for islanders wanting to visit Kirkwall for medical purposes and architectural students from the main island paying a visit to important sites.

Because the journey time is so short, many experts believe the route would lend itself to electric aircraft and expect this to be explored as the technology develops. There has also been talk of linking these two remote islands with a bridge, a move that would surely threaten the existence of the ferry route and the world's shortest flight. But as yet, no plans have been

submitted and so these two beautiful islands remain proud custodians of the world's shortest commercial flight. To look at timetables and book your own short journey, go to www. loganair.co.uk.

101

Dates from
1600s

Number of witch marks hundreds

Deterring
evil spirits,
witches, the devil

Years used
300

HEAD INSIDE A CAVE HOUSING THE BIGGEST COLLECTION OF WITCH MARKS IN THE COUNTRY

CRESWELL CRAGS

Nestled in a quiet corner of the Midlands, where the counties of Nottinghamshire and Derbyshire meet, a series of inland limestone caves house record-breaking secrets for you to discover. Creswell Crags is an unassuming visitor attraction, understated and unpretentious and yet incredibly important and informative. Hidden inside the caves are glimpses into the past, both prehistoric and more recent. Book ahead to get on one of the fabulously educational tours and get ready to enter a subterranean historical paradise.

During the last Ice Age, Creswell Crags were pretty close to the ice sheet that had slowly extended south during the long period of cold weather. The caves were about as far north as humans could live at that time. They took shelter from the elements and on some of the walls they etched simple drawings depicting life at the time. These are the most northerly examples of cave art in Europe, created at a time when those living here were on the dangerous cusp of survival and death. The

record-breaking northern cave art pulls in history buffs from all over and the brilliant guided tour is well worth getting involved with, but it is not the only reason to come here. The other, much more sinister and darker, secrets contained within the caves at Creswell Crags were discovered completely by accident.

A pair of heritage cave experts had enjoyed a tour of Creswell Crags and were chatting to staff in the visitor centre before leaving. One

of them commented that the witch marks in the cave were great examples but nobody at Creswell knew what they were talking about. The resulting conversation led to a detailed university study and ultimately confirmation that the witch marks were genuine. And not only that – this was declared to be by far the biggest collection of such markings in the country and one of the biggest in the world. There were so many of the 'VV' etchings in the cave that it dwarfed some of the most significant discoveries that had gone before.

So just what are witch marks? These curious cave scratchings – apotropaic marks – date back to the 17th century, a much more superstitious time when there was genuine fear within communities about being cursed by evil spirits and the resulting hardship that could wreak havoc on their lives, maybe through

illness, lack of water or failing crops. To try to ward off these evil spirits, to combat witchcraft, or maybe even deter the devil himself, a trend was started around Creswell to etch 'VV' in the walls of the cave – thought to stand for Virgo Virginum, the Virgin Mary.

It turns out there were hundreds of these markings left on the walls at Creswell, with experts thinking people came from all over the region, over a period of three centuries, all trying to allay their fears and stop bad things from happening. A key difference between Creswell and other cave sites with witch marks is quite ominous. Usually the marks were etched at the entrance to the cave, but these are placed deeper inside, beside a gap going further underground. Just what were these superstitious people of yesteryear trying to keep down in the bowels of the earth?

INDEX

PHOTO CREDITS